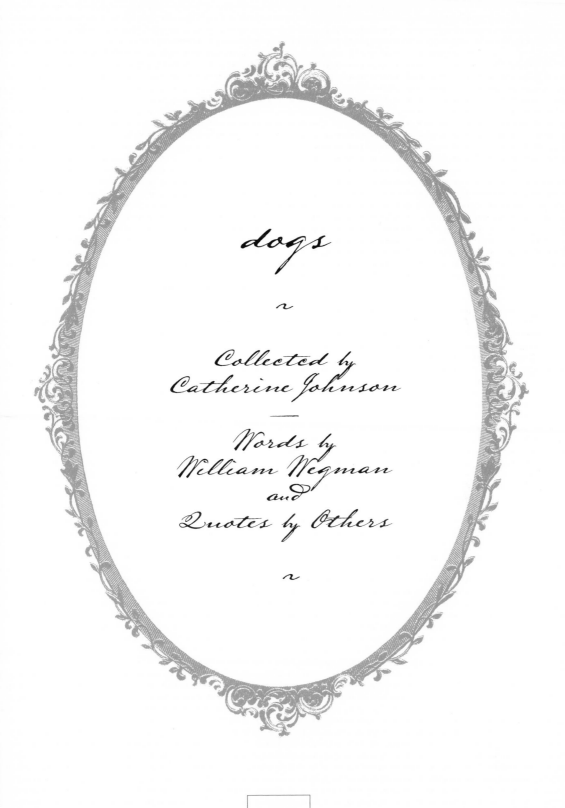

# dogs

~

Collected by
Catherine Johnson

—

Words by
William Wegman
and
Quotes by Others

~

Φ

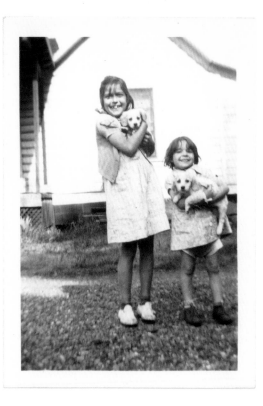

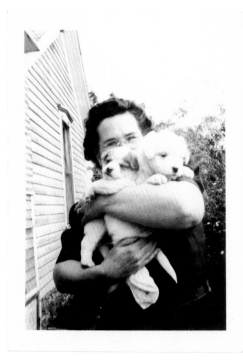

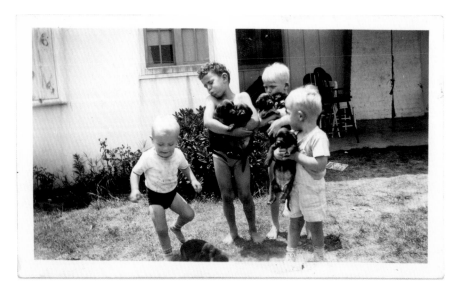

There is no
psychiatrist in the
world like a puppy.
— Ben Williams

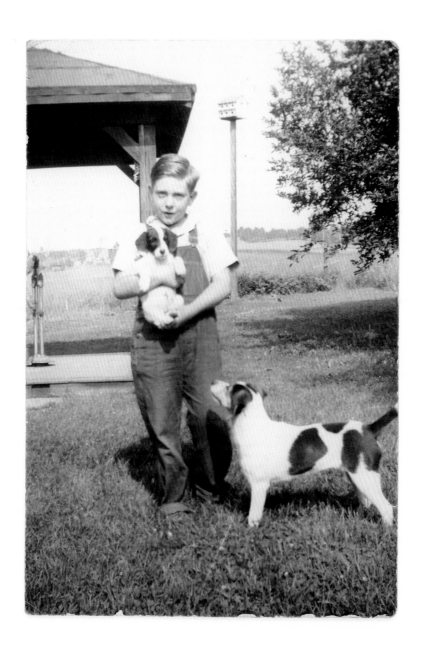

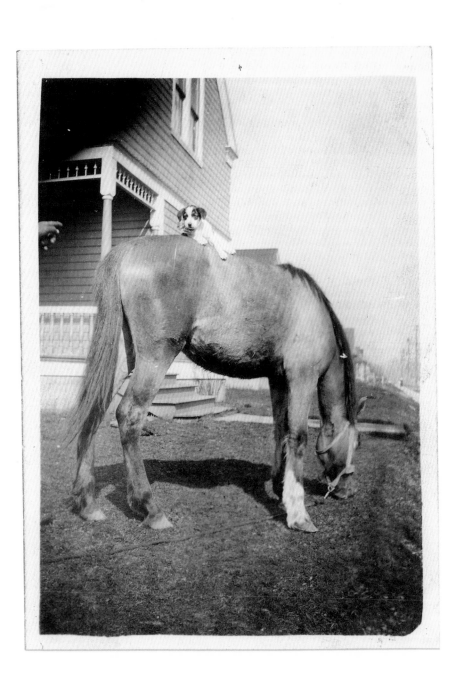

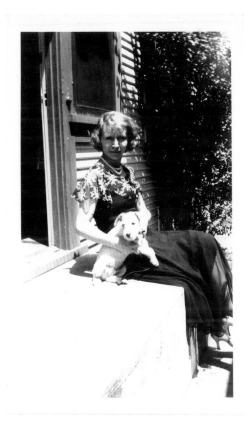

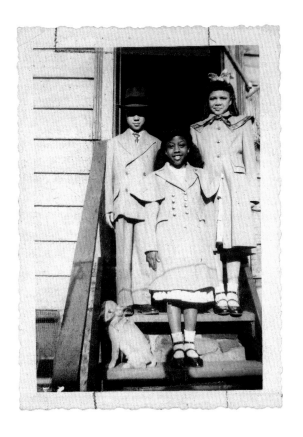

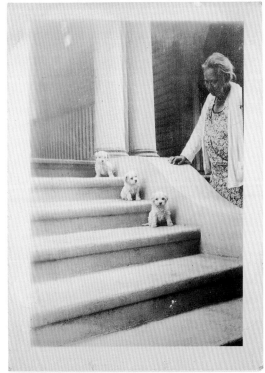

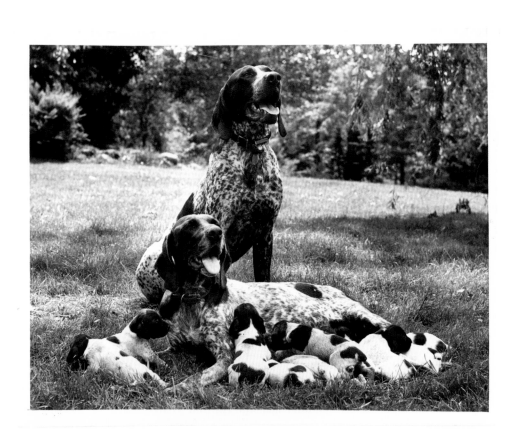

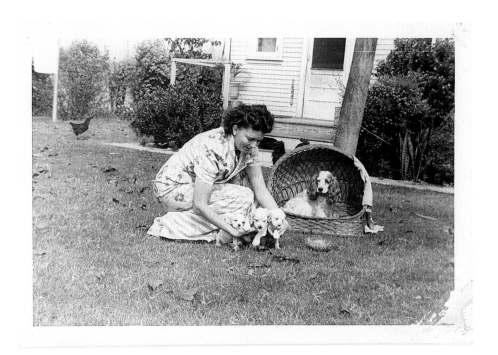

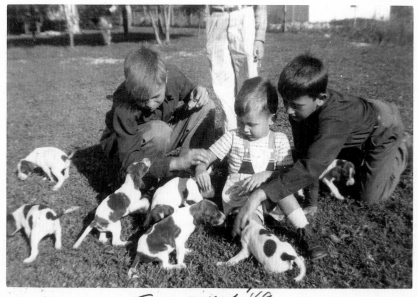

august '49

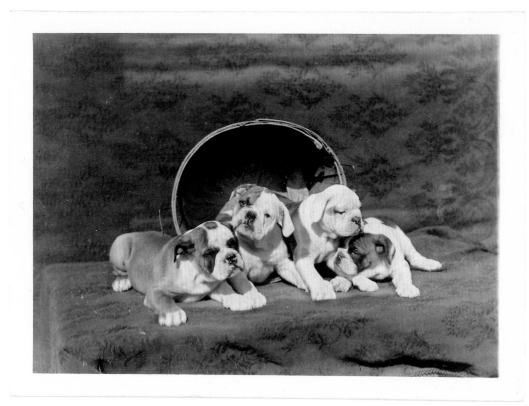

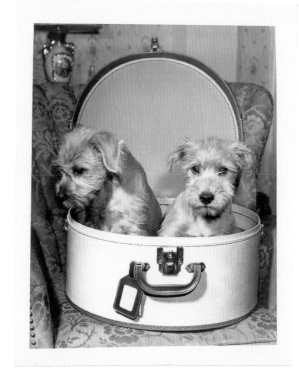

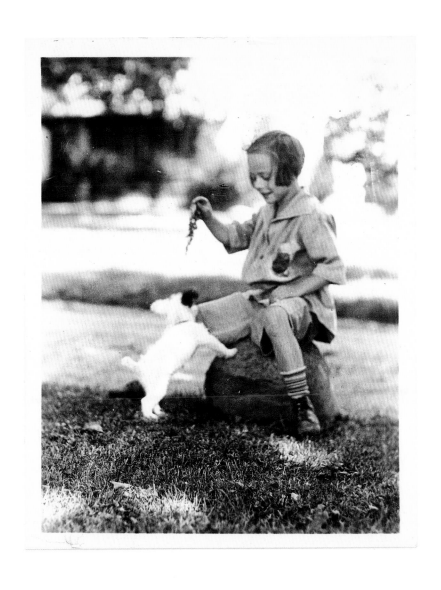

*If you think dogs can't count, try
putting three dog biscuits in your pocket
and then giving Fido only two of them.*
*— Phil Pastoret*

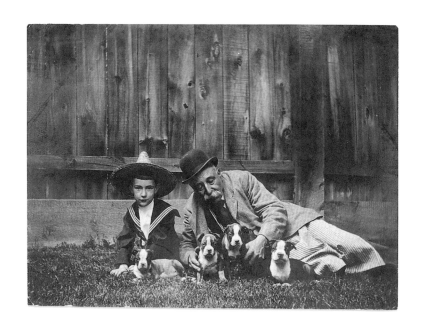

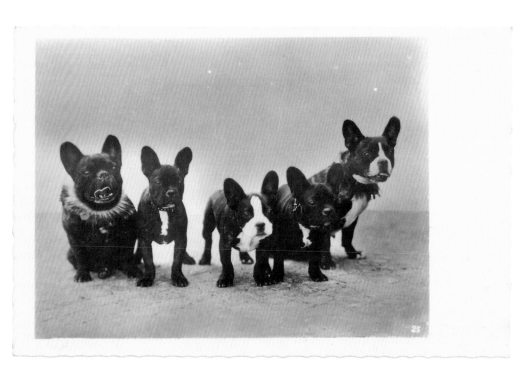

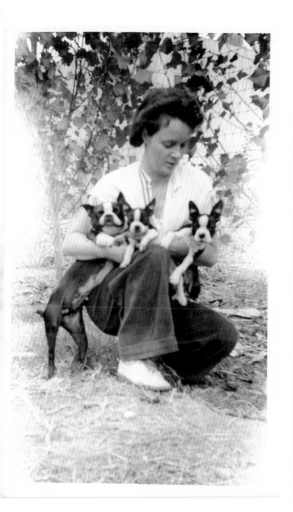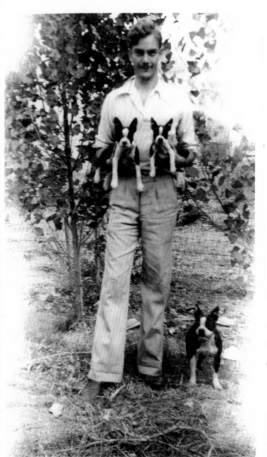

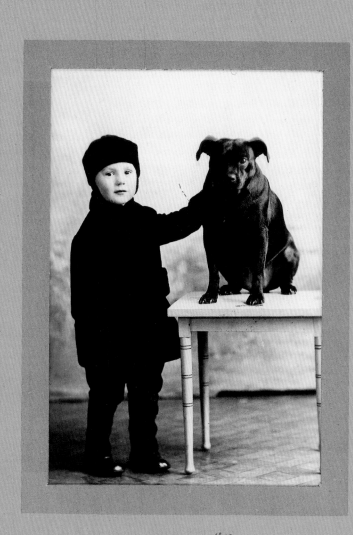

The Park Studio
10 PARK ST.
GLENS FALLS, N.Y.

*Every puppy should have a boy.*
— Erma Bombeck

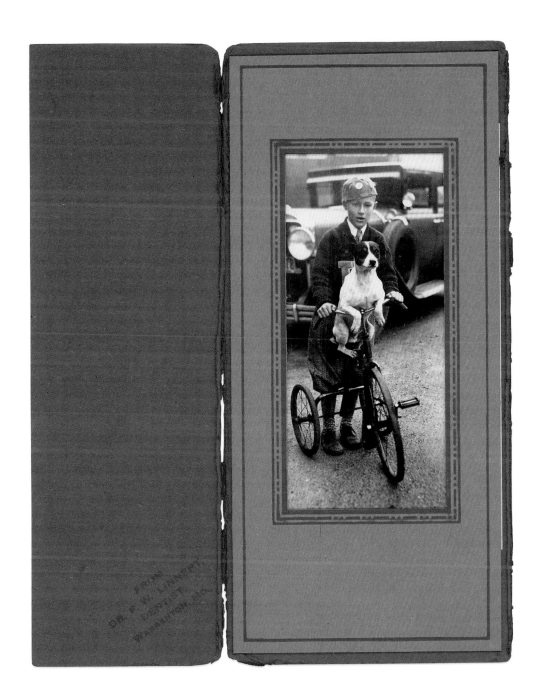

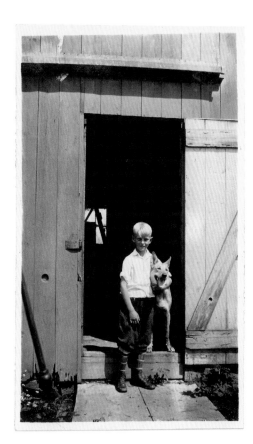
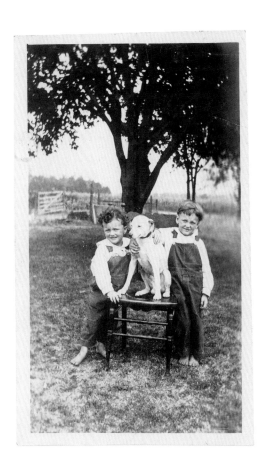
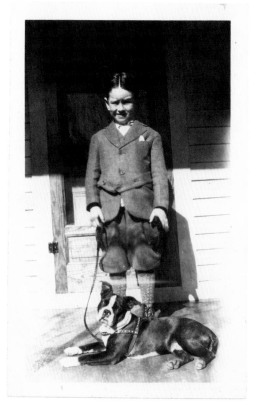

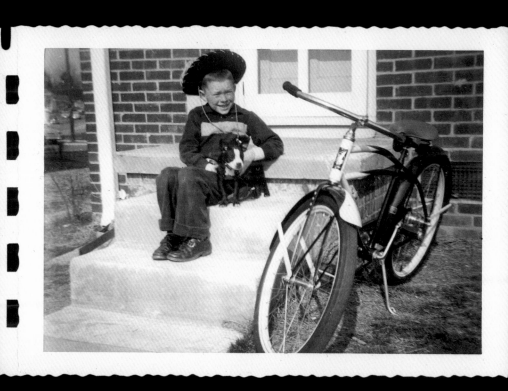

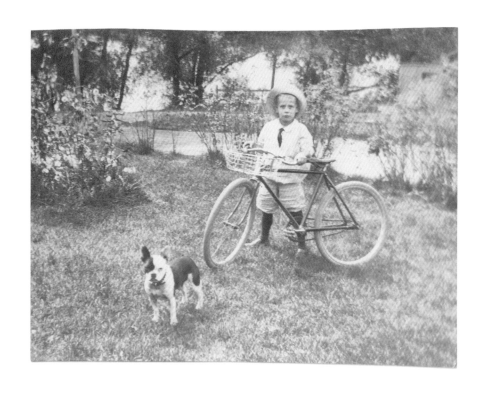

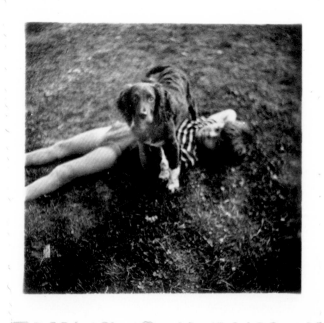

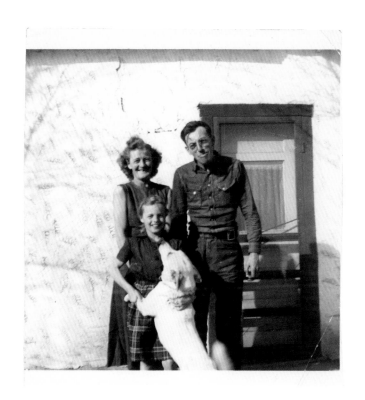

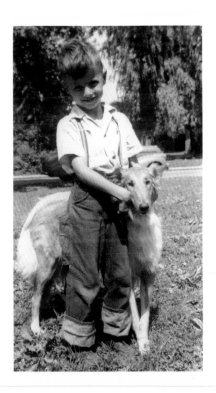

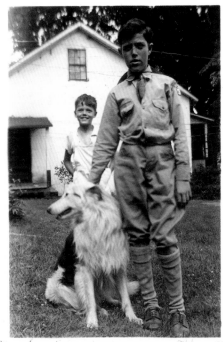

Bob dog king, miller

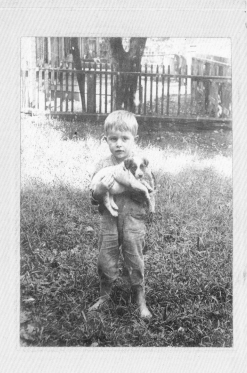

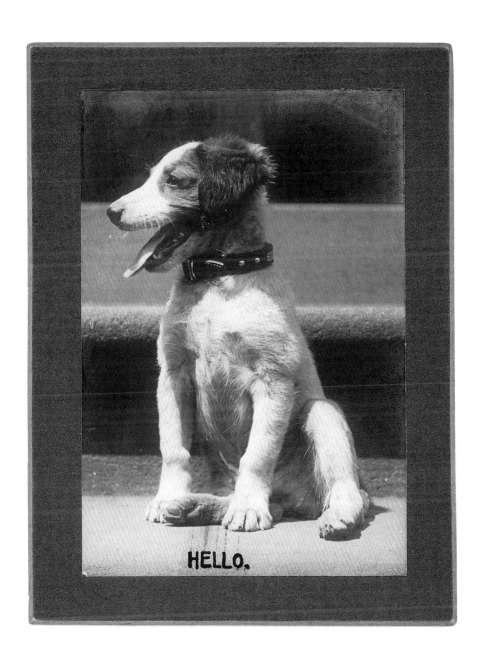

HELLO.

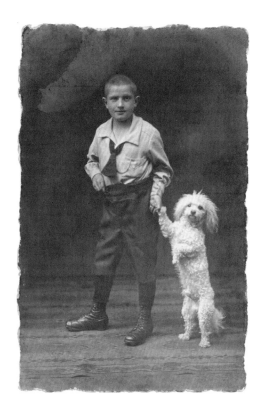

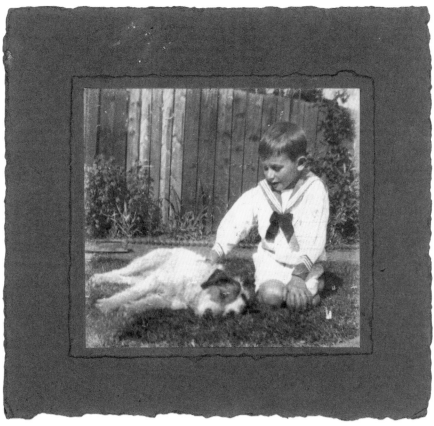

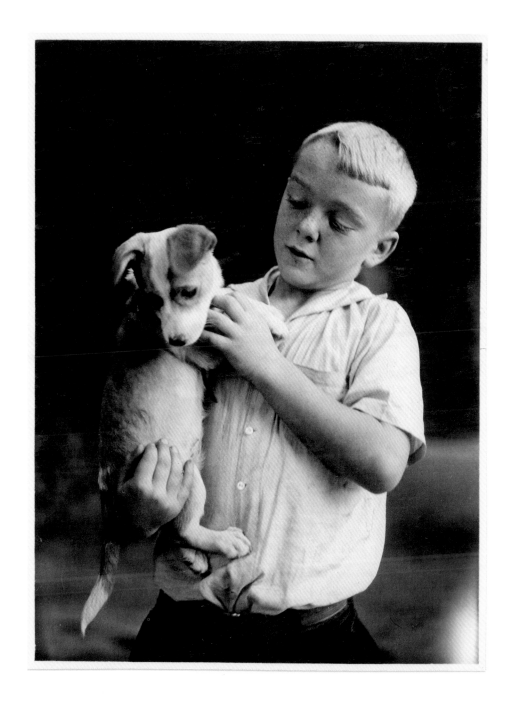

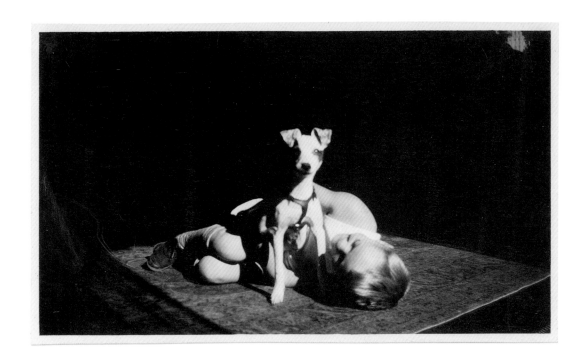

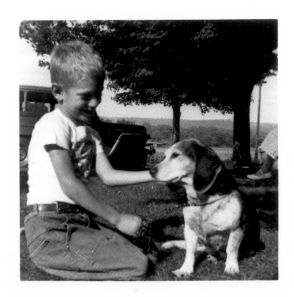

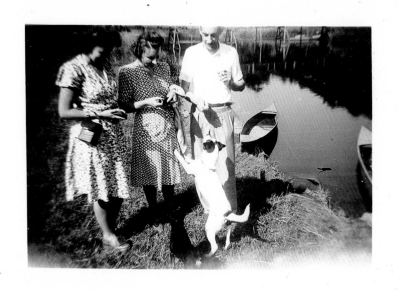

A dog can express more
with his tail in minutes
than his owner can express
with his tongue in hours.
— Anonymous

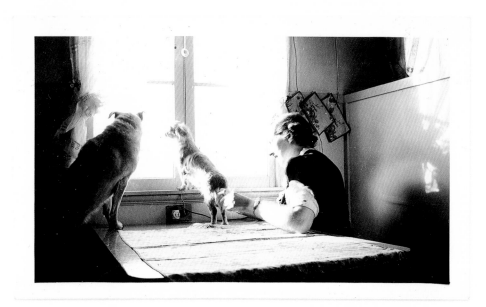
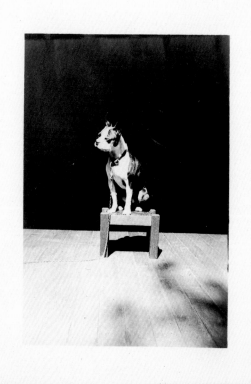
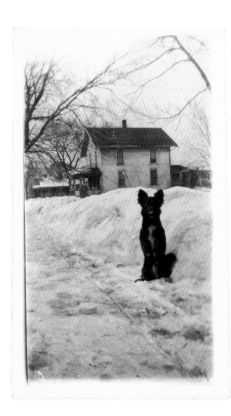

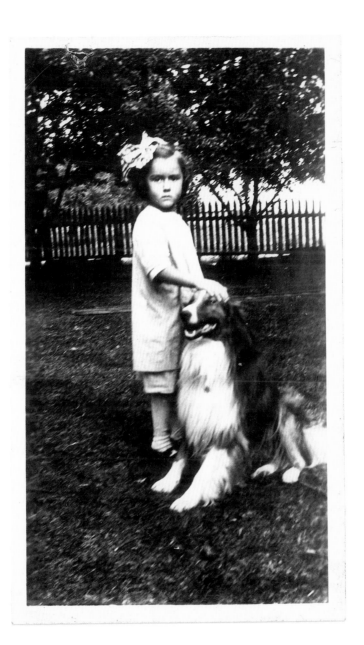

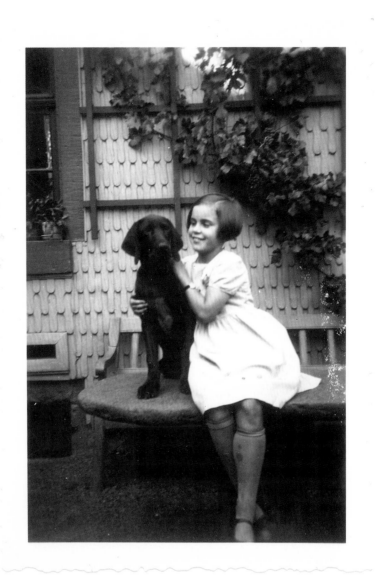

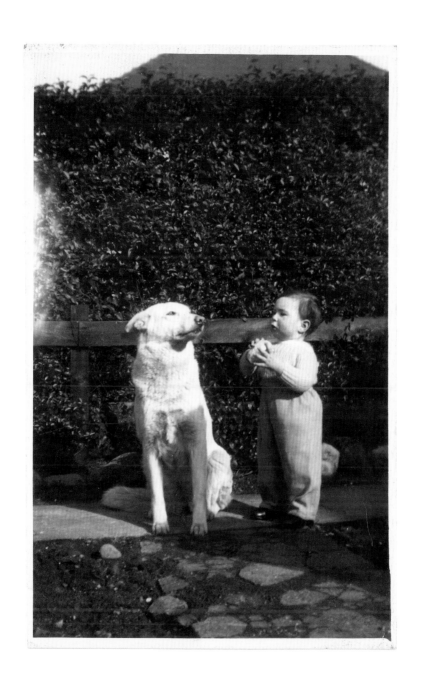

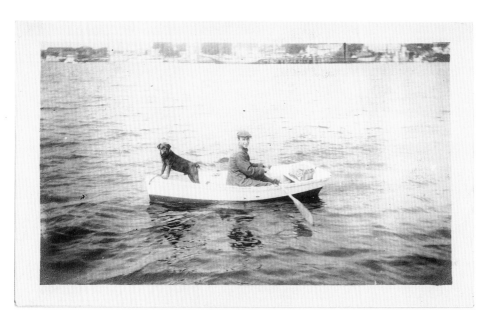

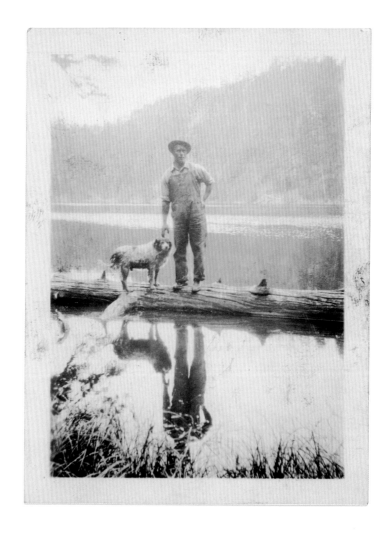

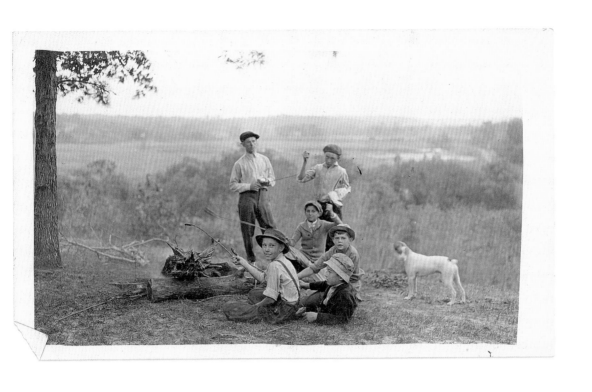

You think dogs will not be in heaven?
I tell you, they will be there
long before any of us.
— Robert Louis Stevenson

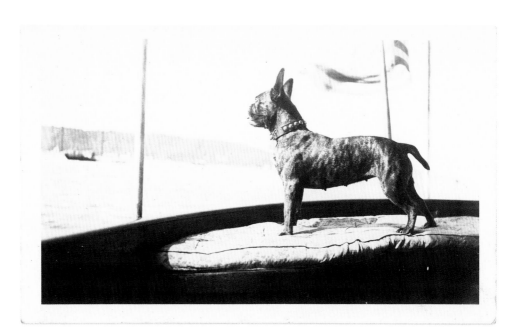

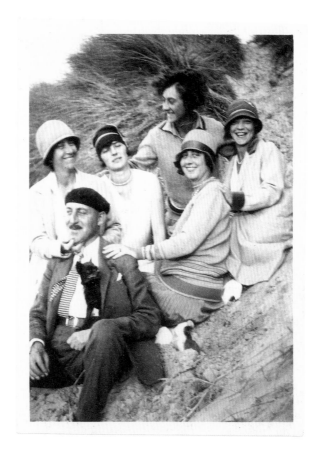

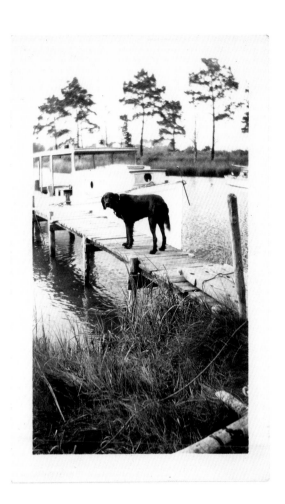

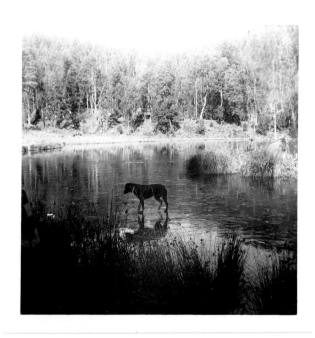

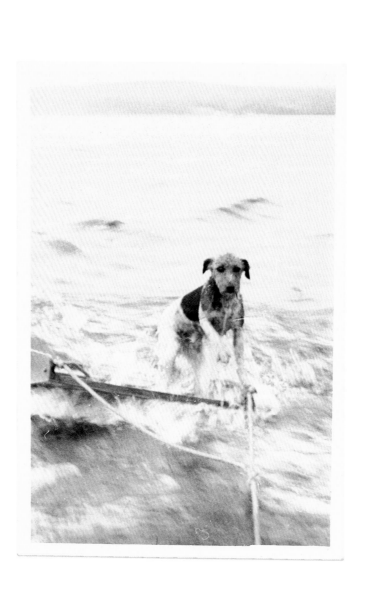

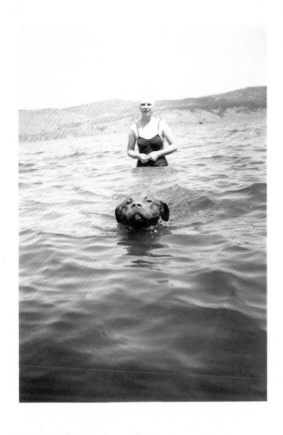

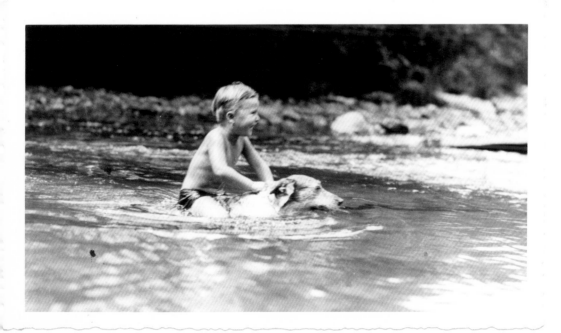

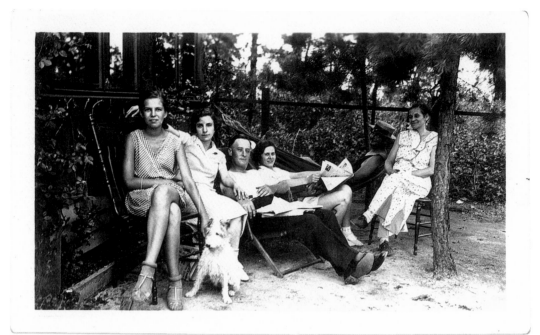

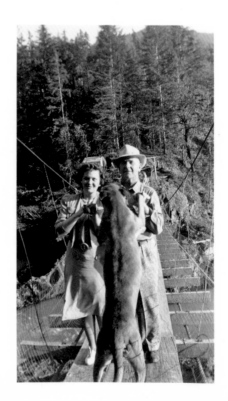

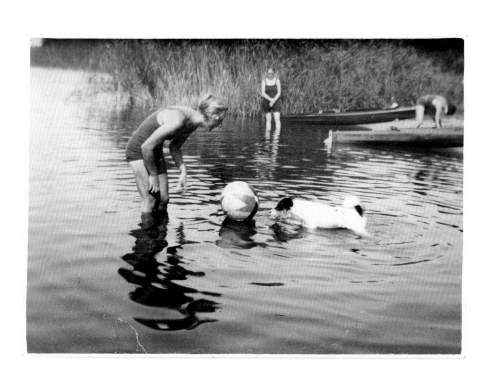

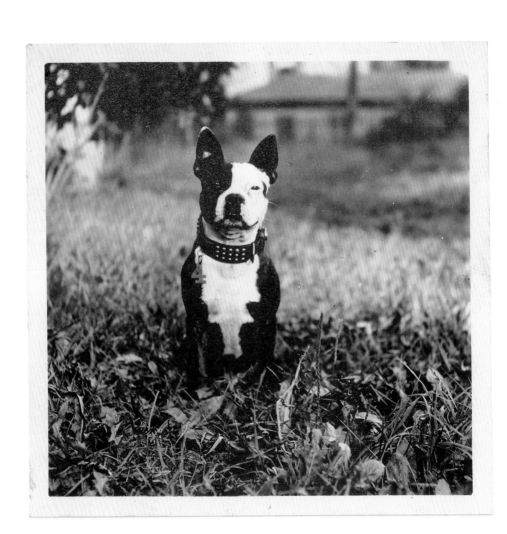

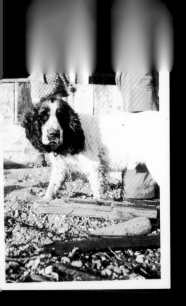

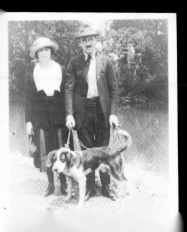

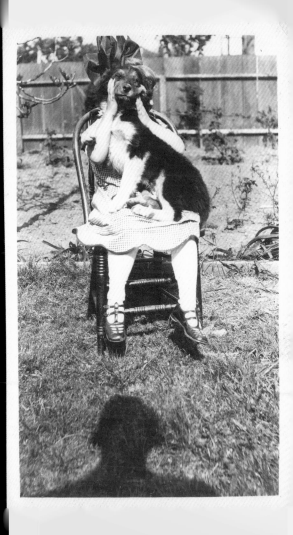

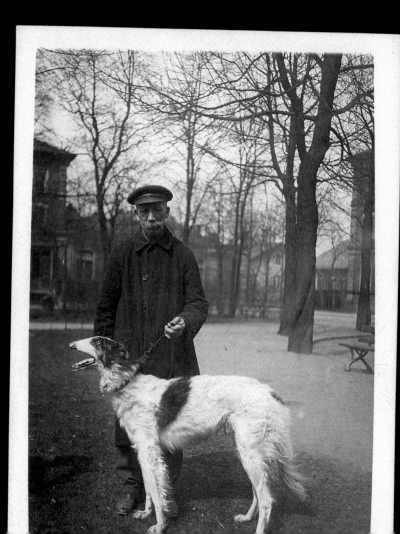

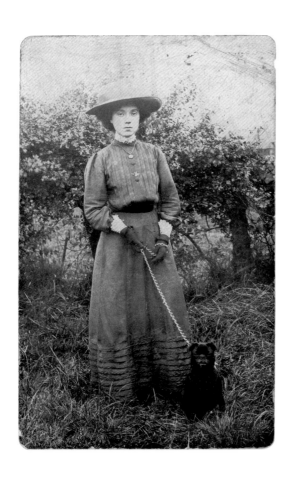

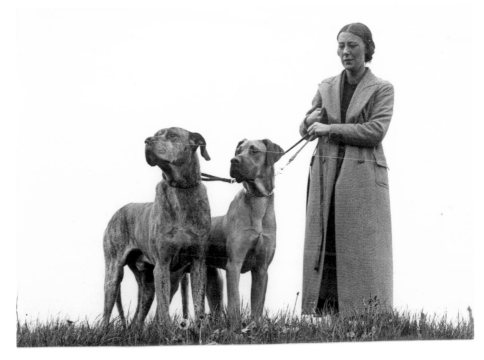

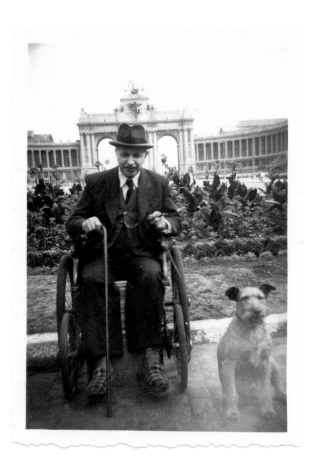

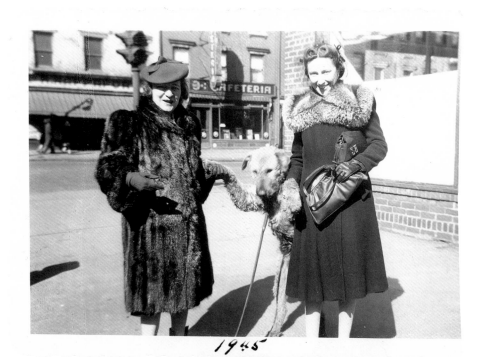

1945

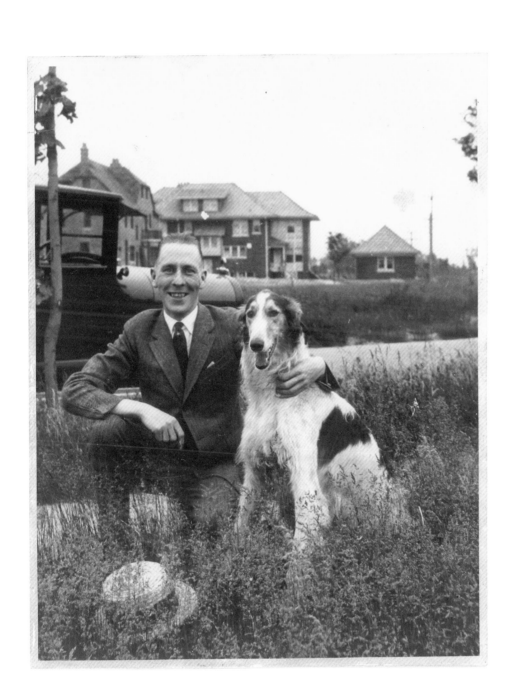

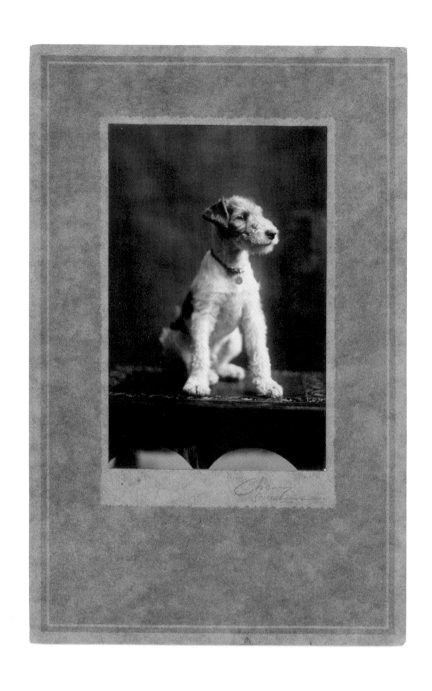

*A dog has the soul of a philosopher.*
— *Plato*

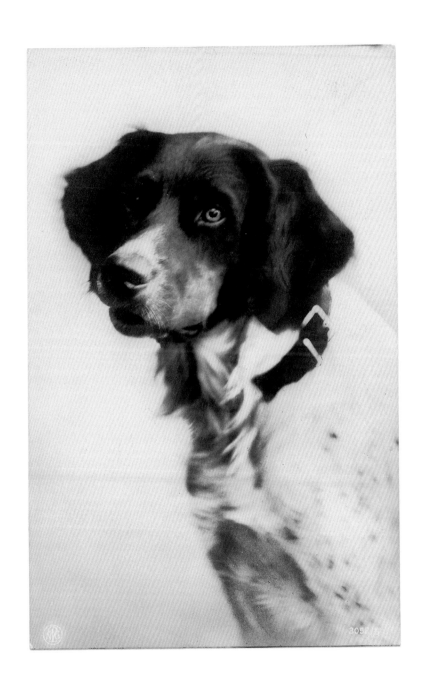

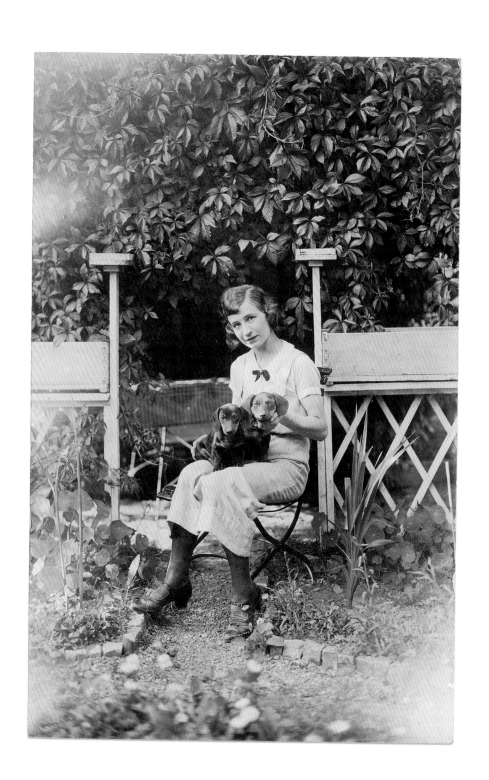

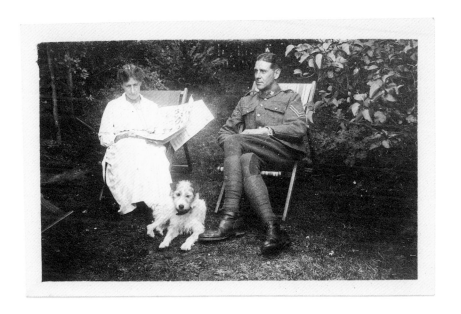

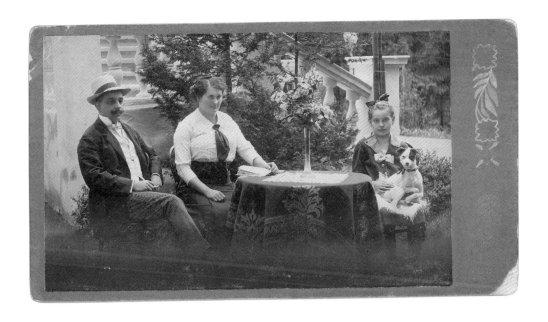

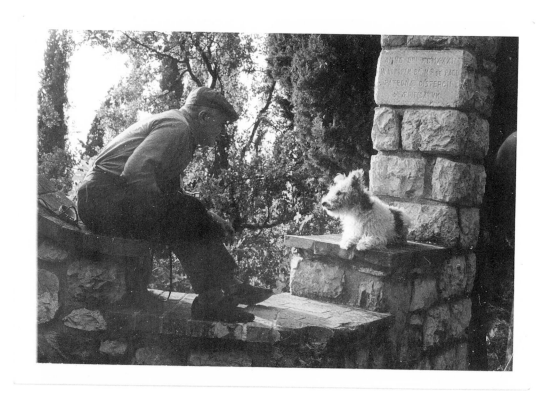

*No one appreciates the very*
*special genius of your conversations*
*as a dog does.*
*— Christopher Morley*

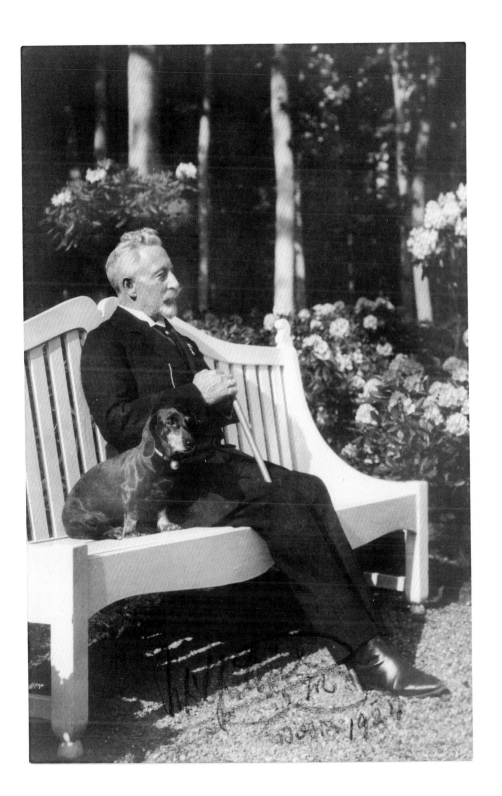

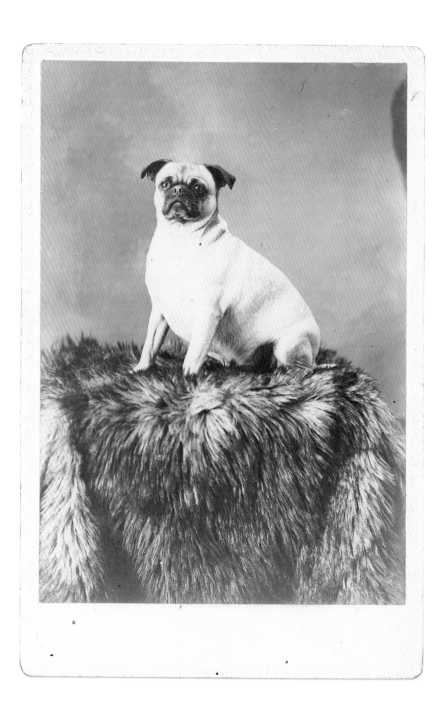

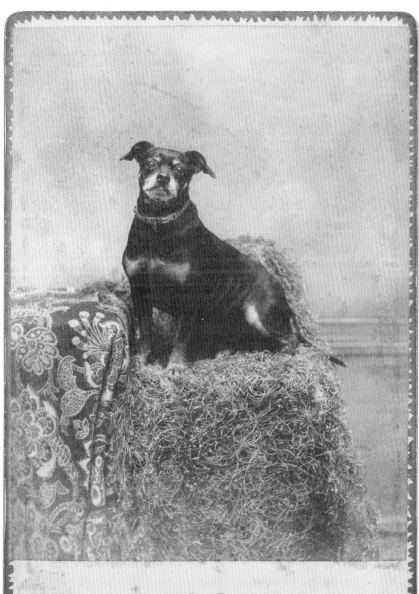

Hughson & Son, St. Joseph, Mich.

*To his dog, every man is Napoleon;*
*hence the constant popularity of dogs.*
*— Aldous Huxley*

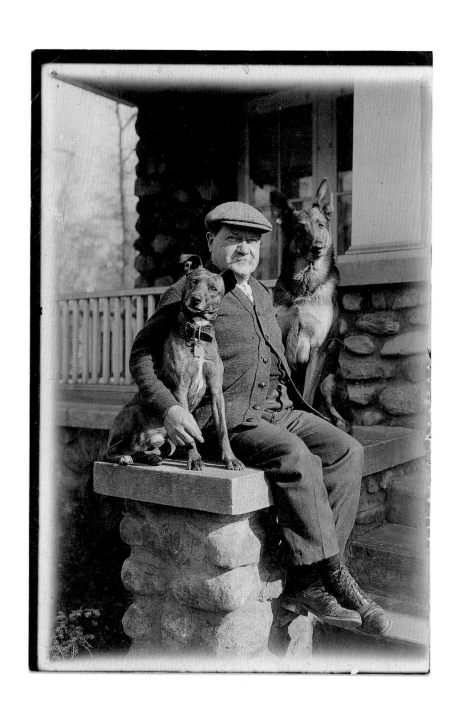

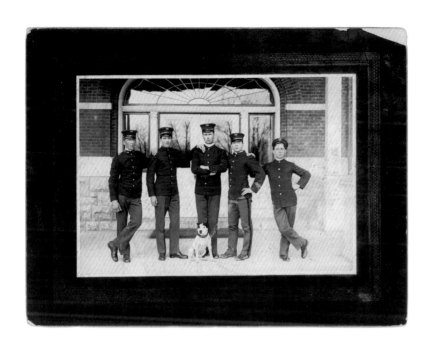

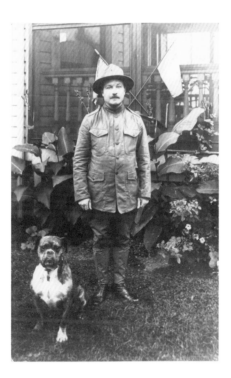

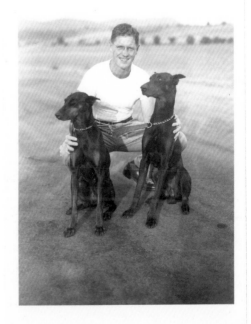

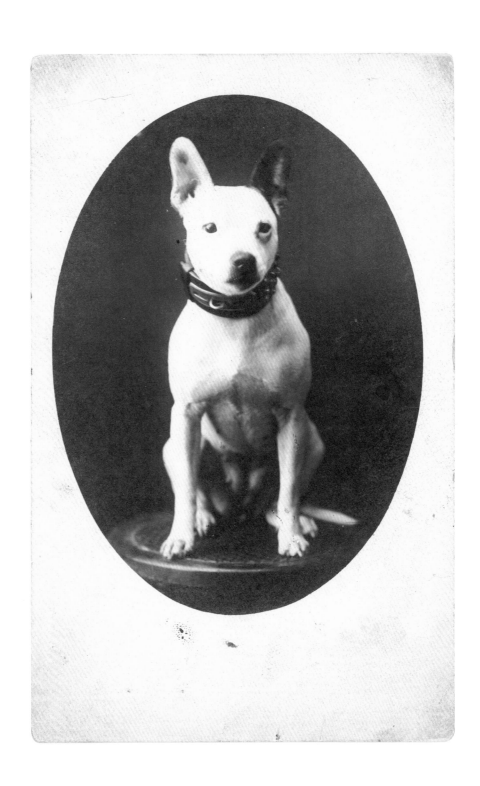

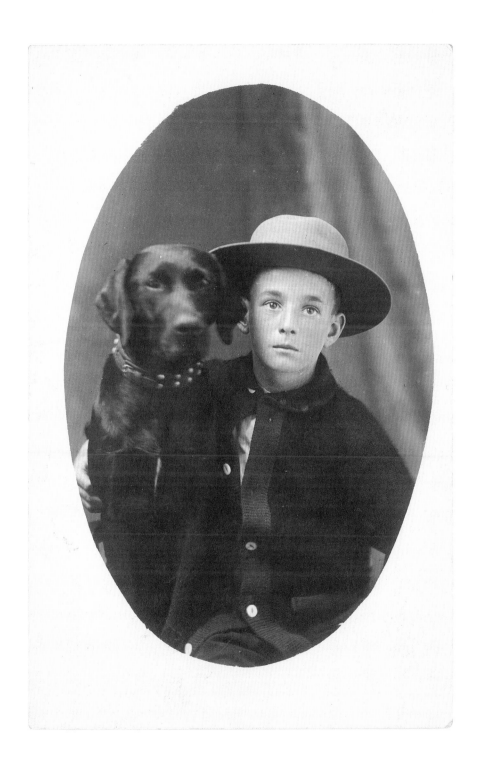

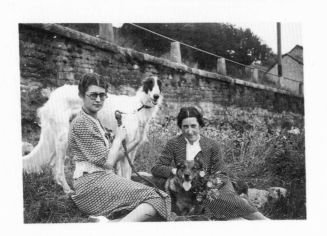

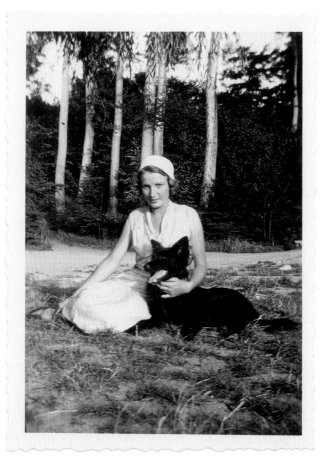

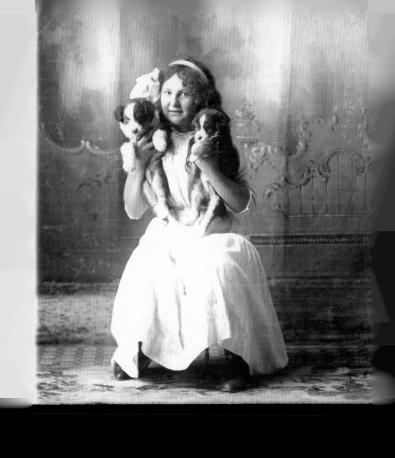
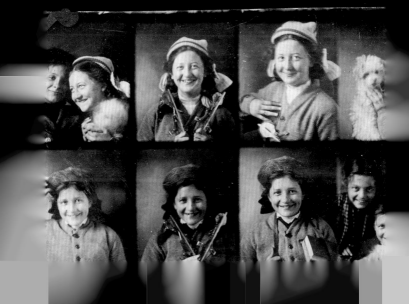

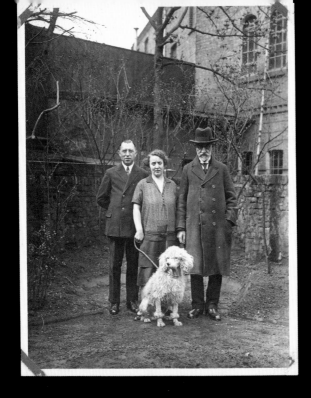

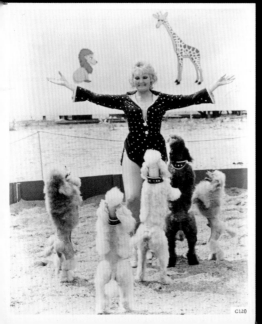

C120

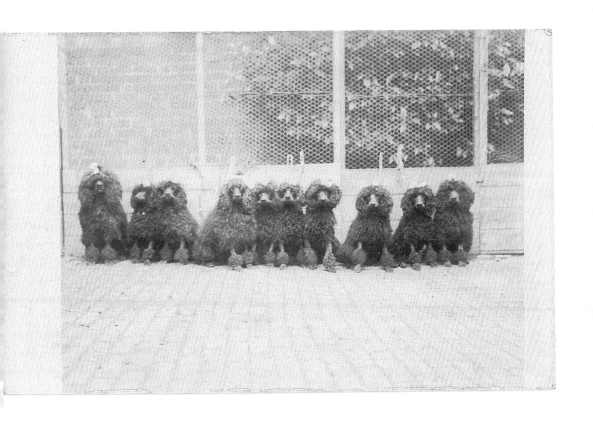

*They're not dogs. They're art.*
*— Rachael Leigh*

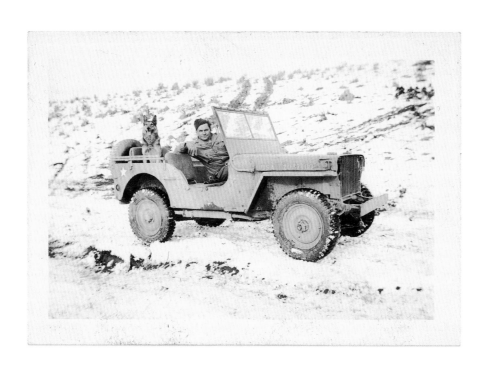

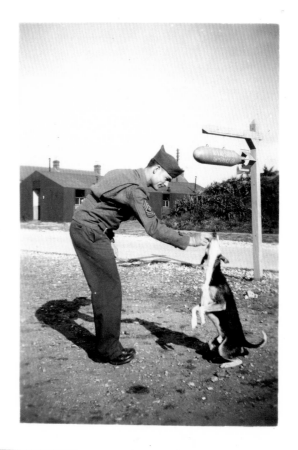

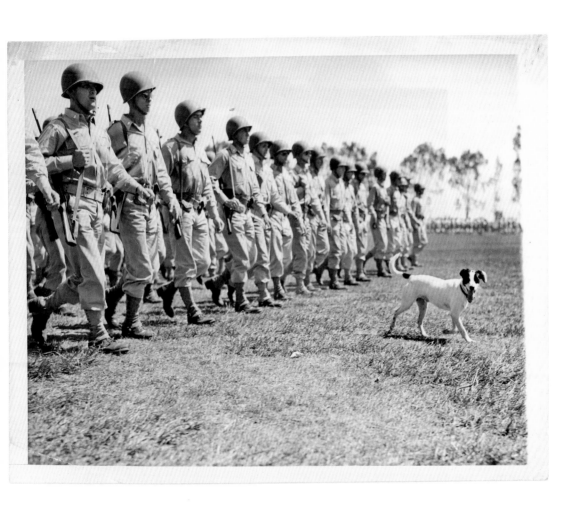

What counts is not necessarily the size of the dog in the fight — it's the size of the fight in the dog.
— Dwight D. Eisenhower

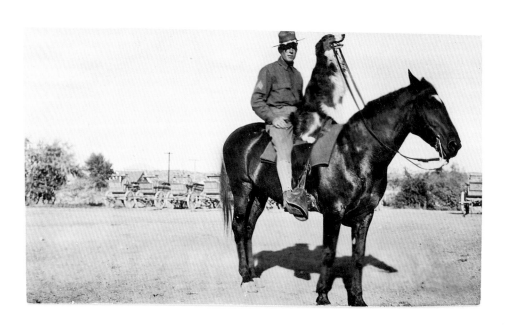

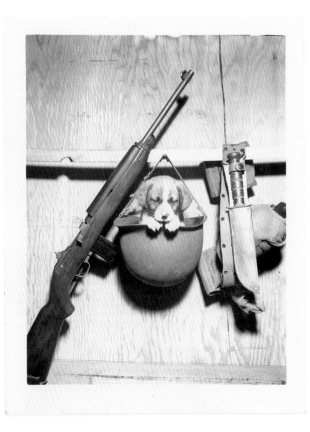

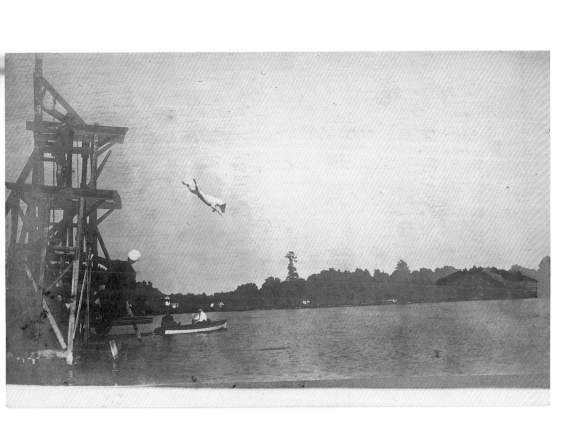

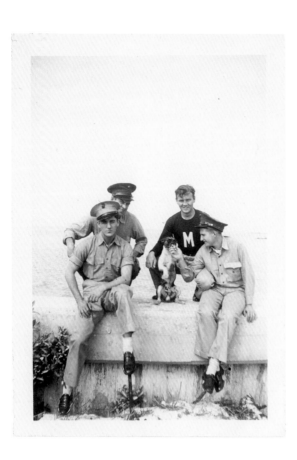

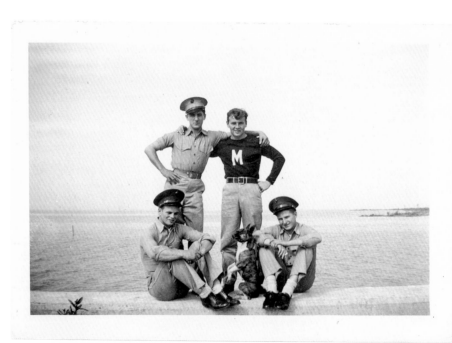

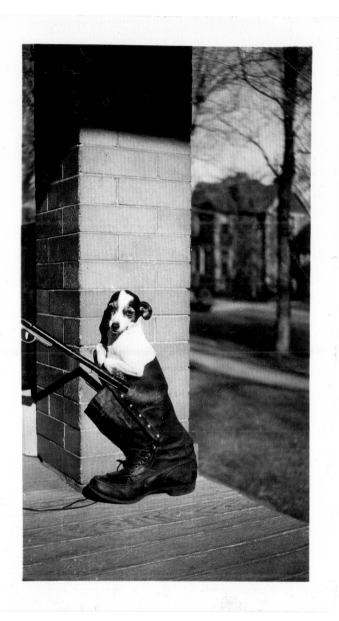

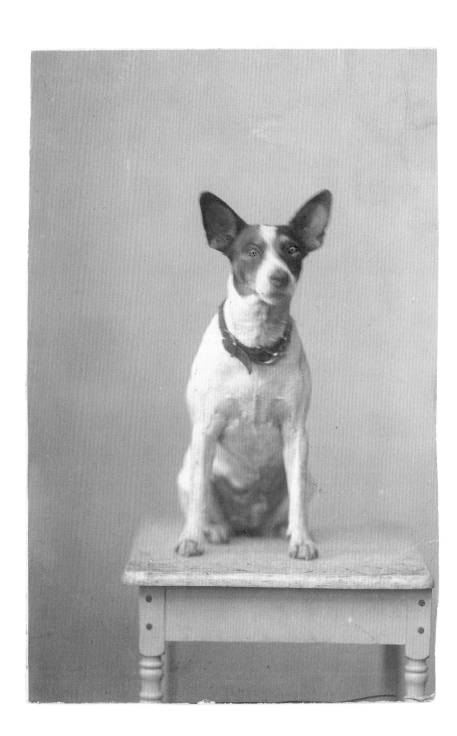

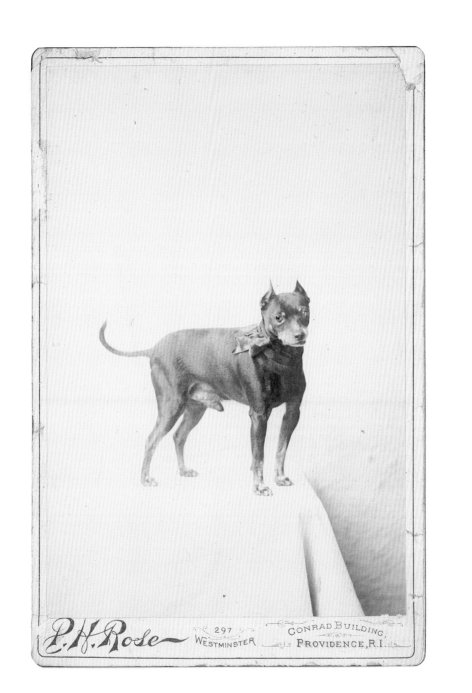

P. H. Rose
297
WESTMINSTER
CONRAD BUILDING,
PROVIDENCE, R.I.

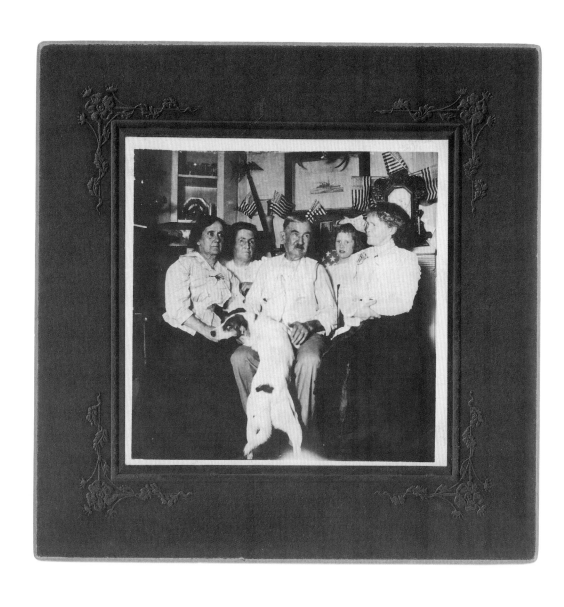

You can't keep a good man down
— or an overly affectionate dog.
— Anonymous

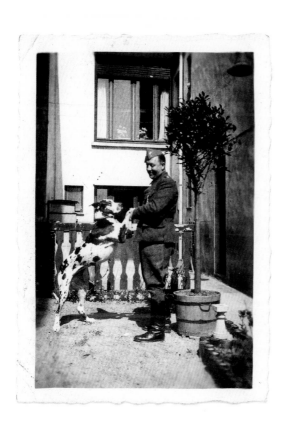

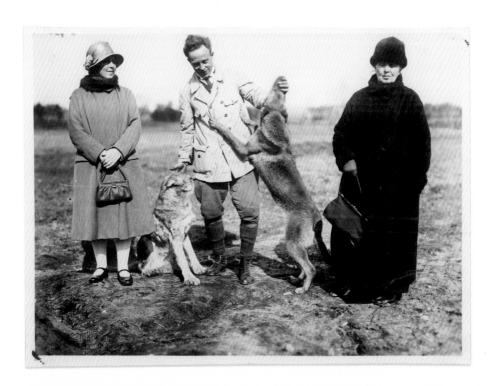

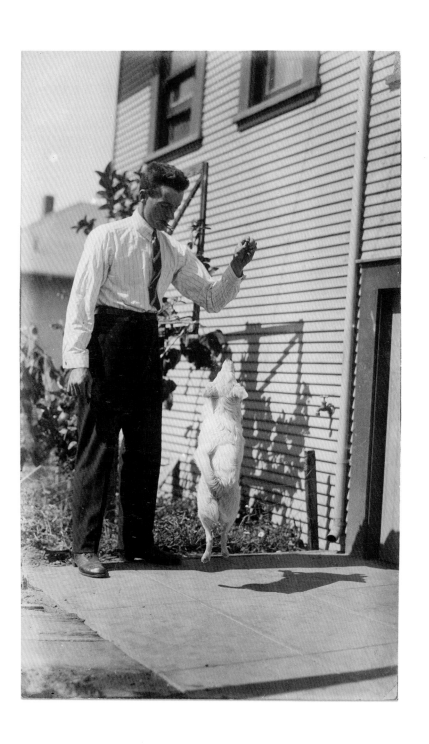

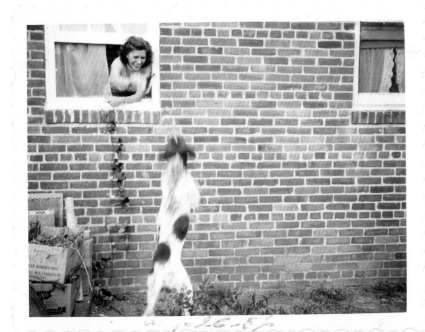

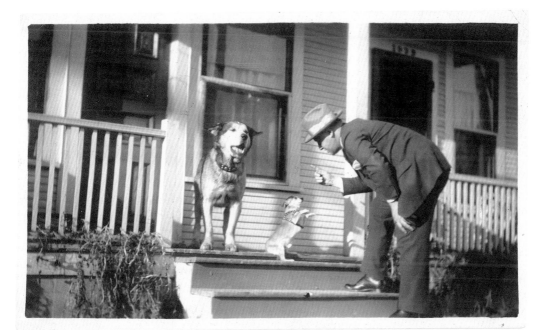

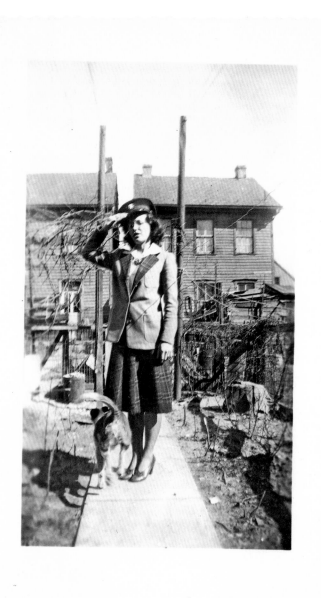

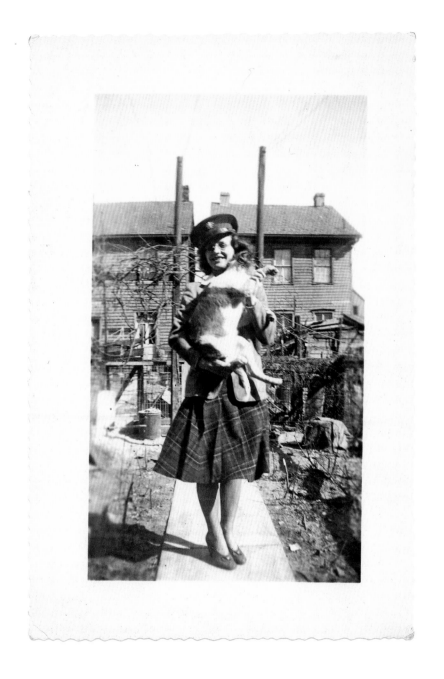

*The more I know about men,
the more I like dogs.
— Gloria Allred*

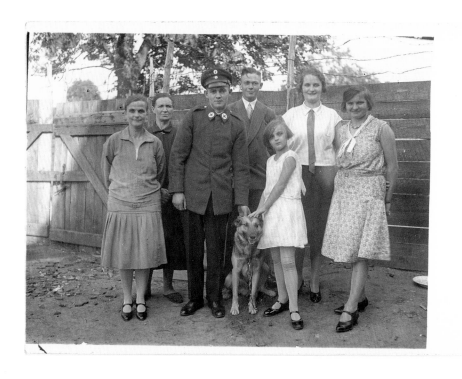

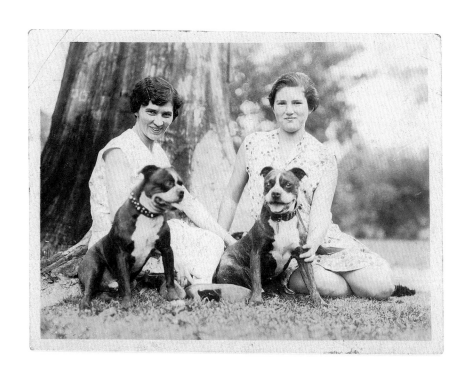

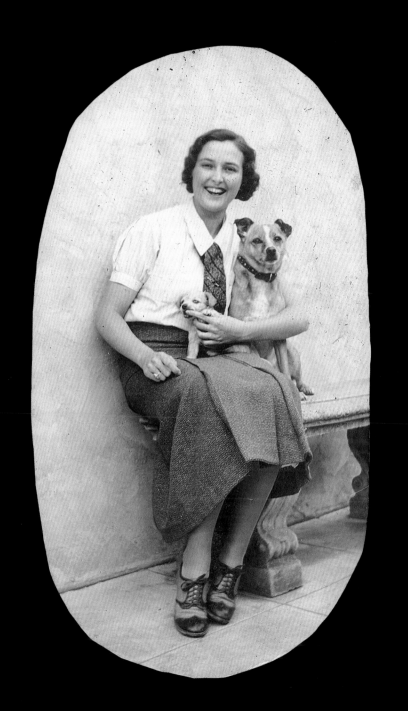

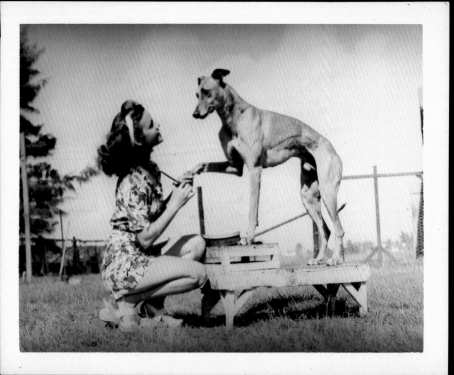

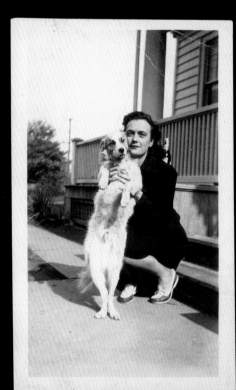

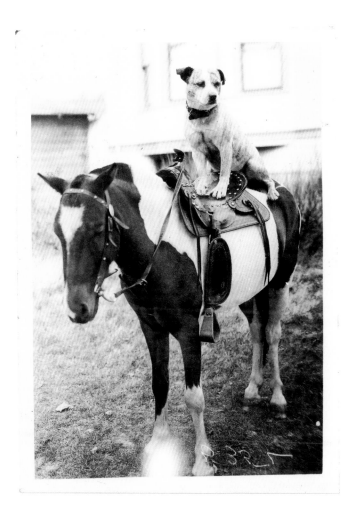

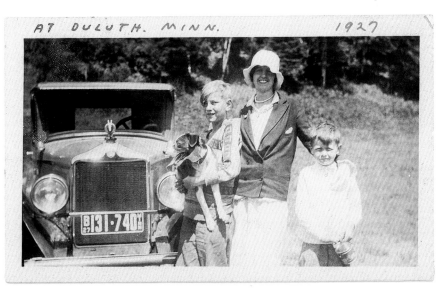

AT DULUTH. MINN. 1927

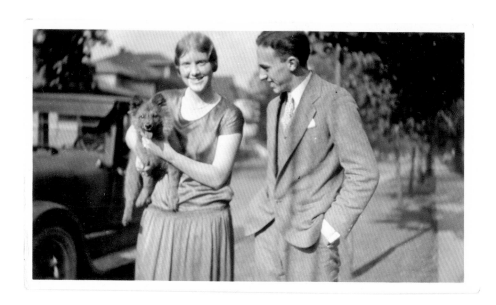

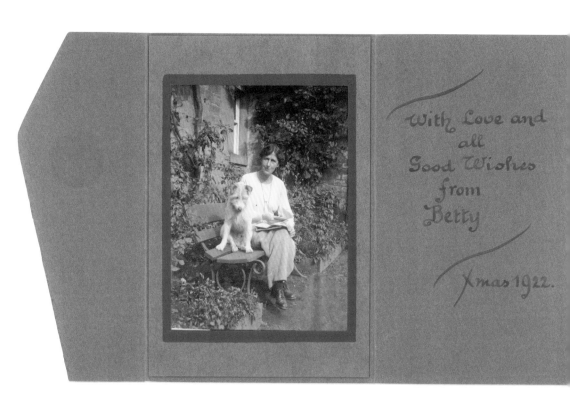

With Love and
all
Good Wishes
from
Betty

Xmas 1922.

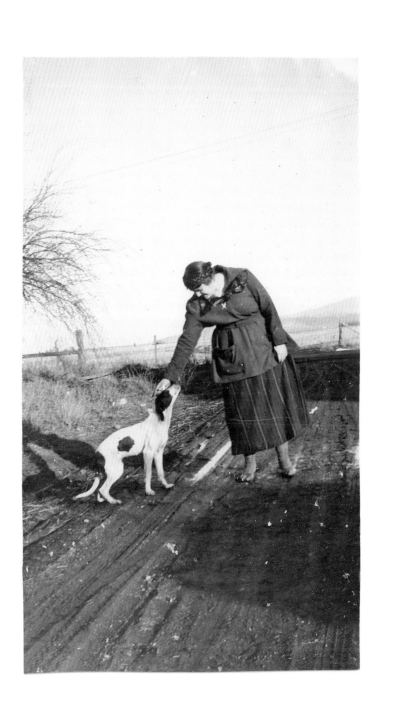

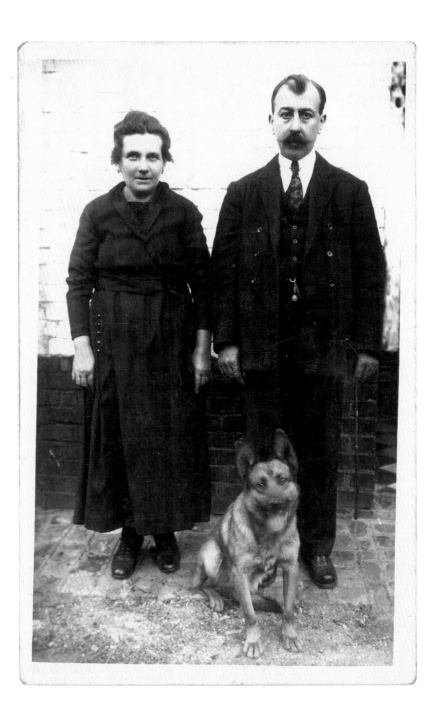

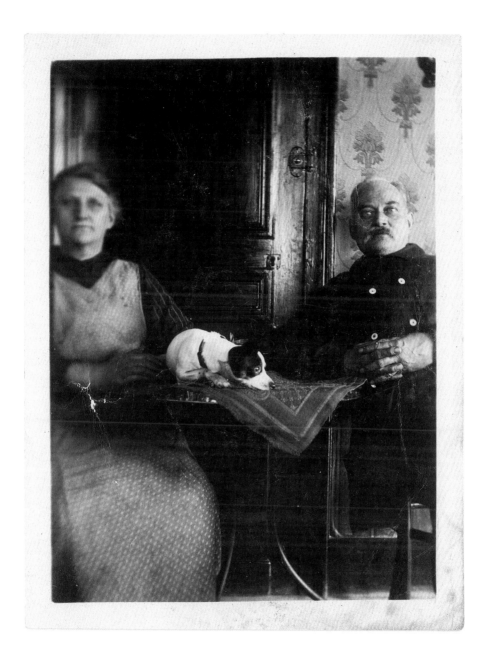

*Acquiring a dog may be the
only opportunity a human ever
has to choose a relative.
— Mordecai Siegal*

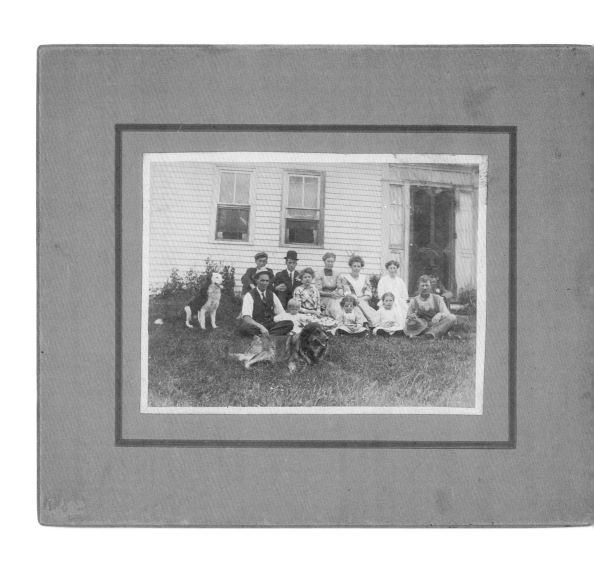

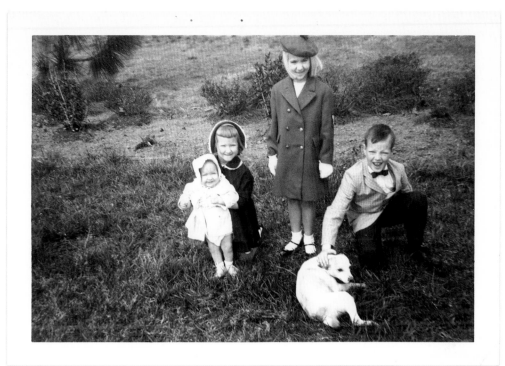

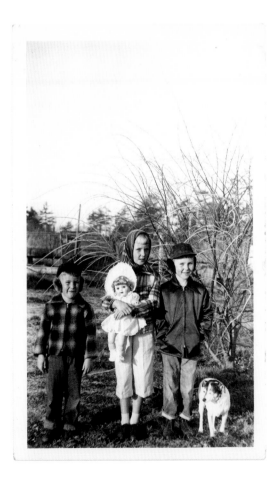

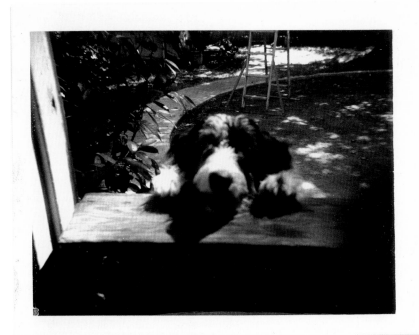

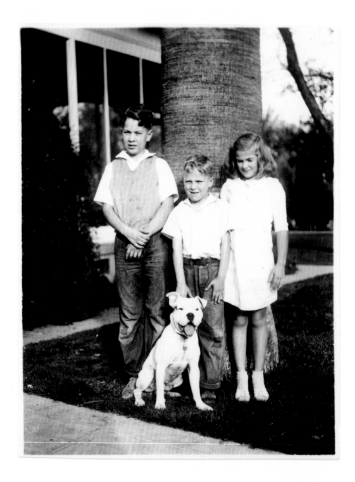

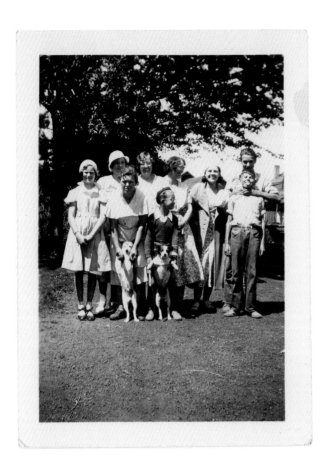

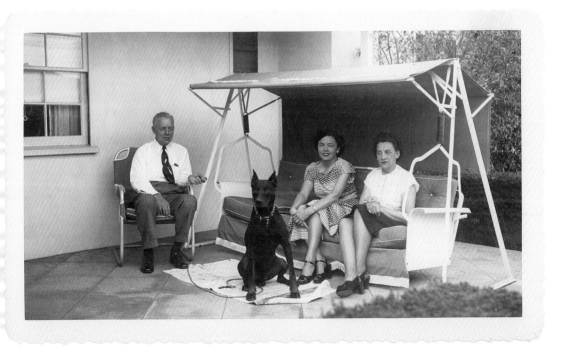

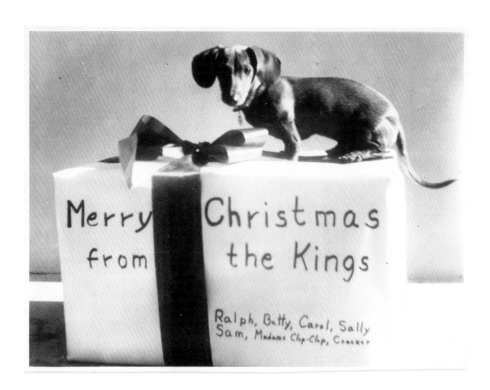

Merry Christmas from the Kings

Ralph, Betty, Carol, Sally
Sam, Madame Chip-Chip, Cracker

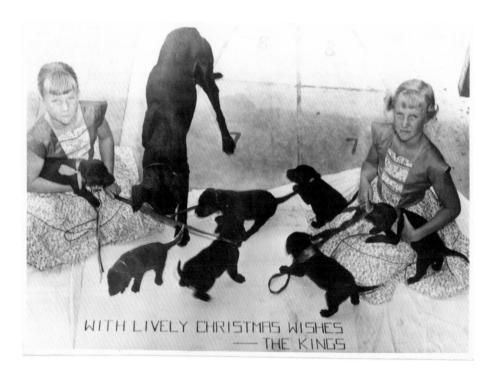

WITH LIVELY CHRISTMAS WISHES
— THE KINGS

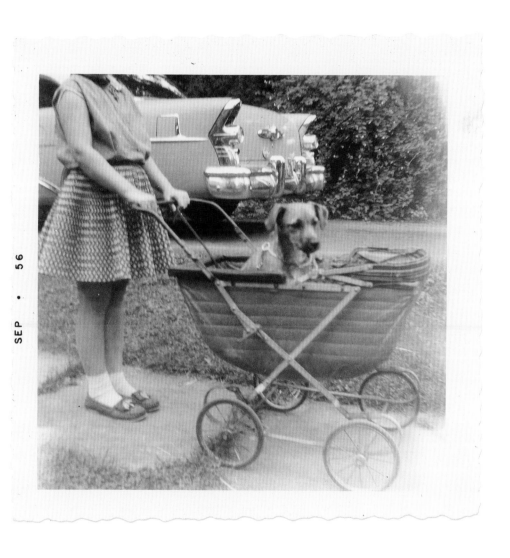

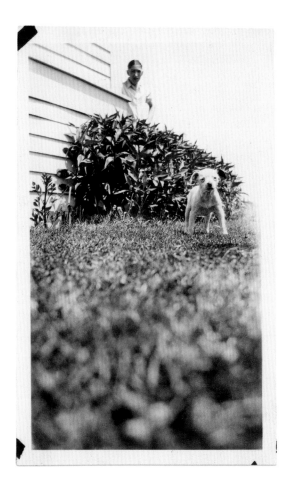
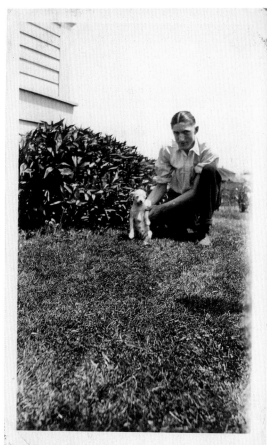

*My little dog — a heartbeat at my feet.*
*— Edith Wharton*

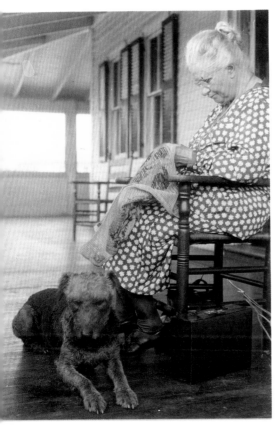 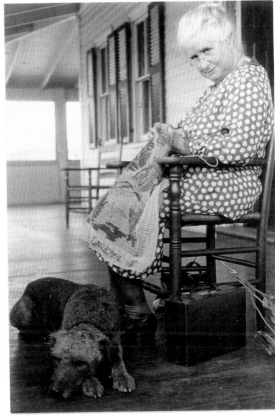

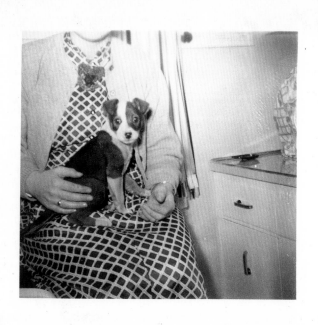

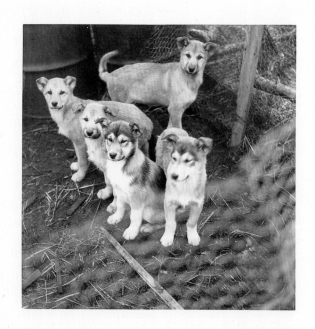

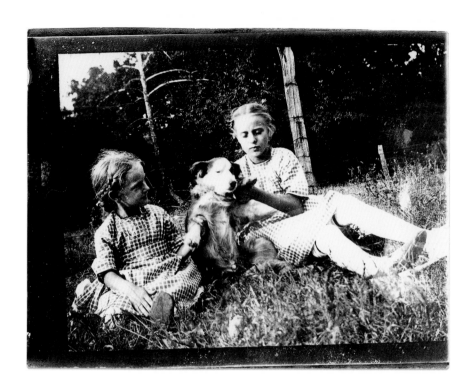

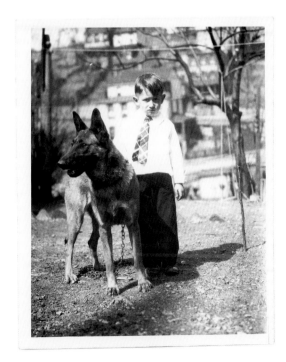

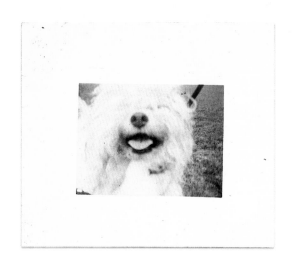

If a dog will not come to you
after having looked you in the
face, you should go home and
examine your conscience.
— Woodrow Wilson

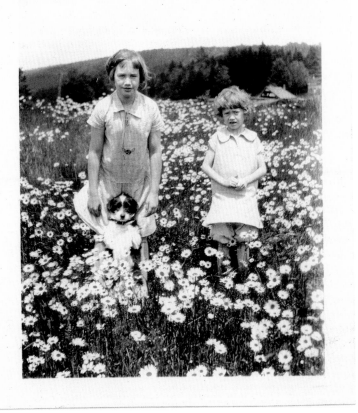

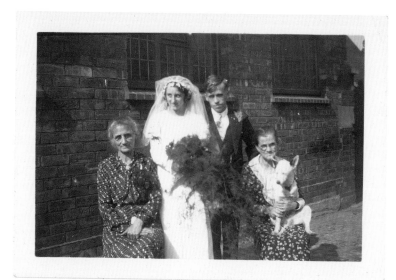

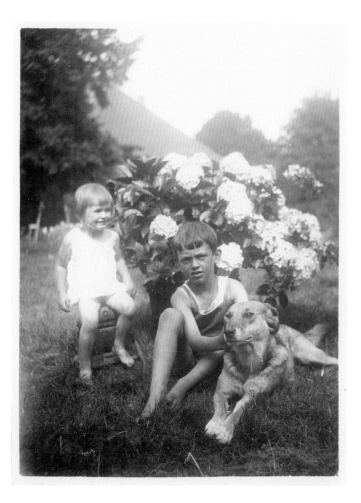

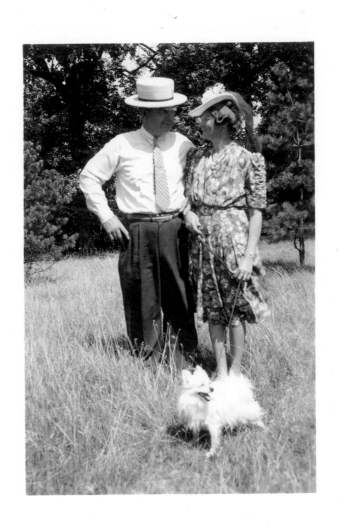

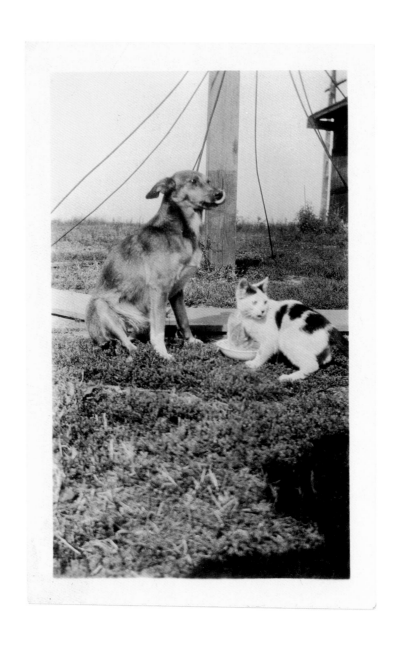

*Curiosity killed the cat,*
*but the dog is still a suspect.*
*— Anonymous*

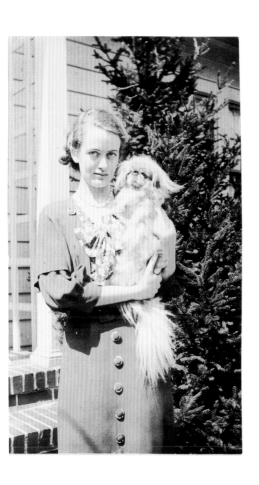

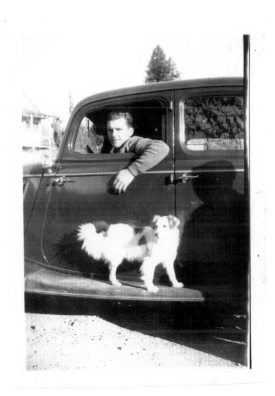

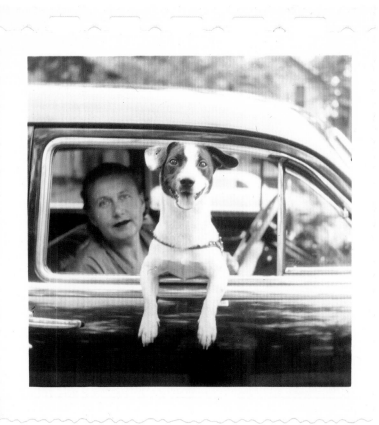

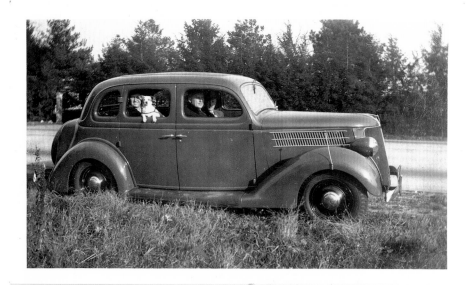

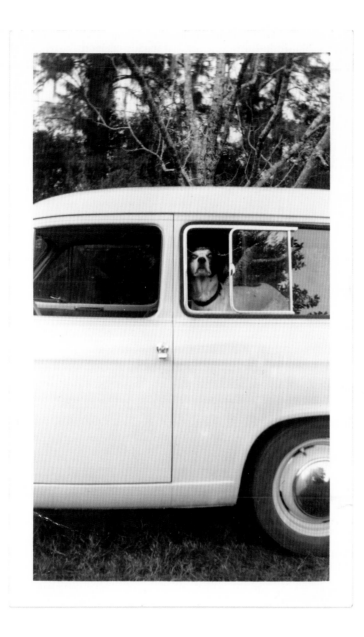

*Did you ever notice when you blow in a dog's face he gets mad at you? But when you take him in a car he sticks his head out the window!*
*— Steve Bluestone*

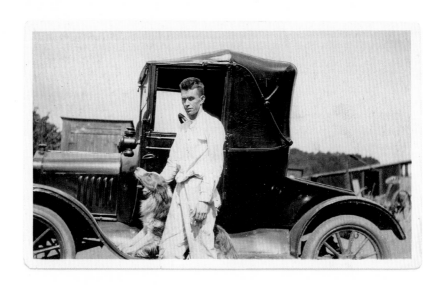

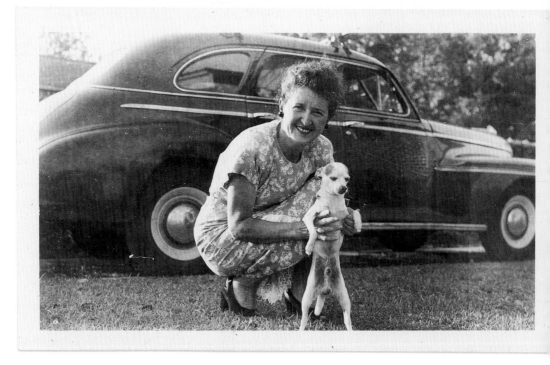

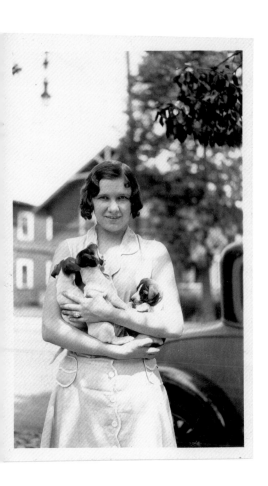

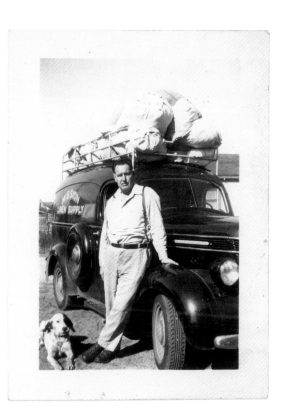

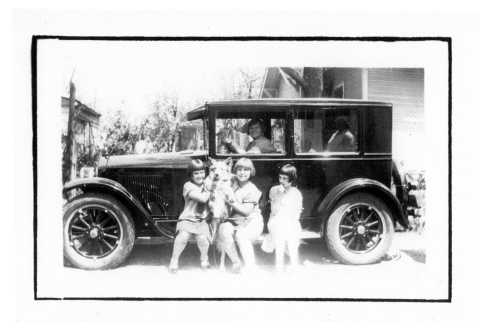

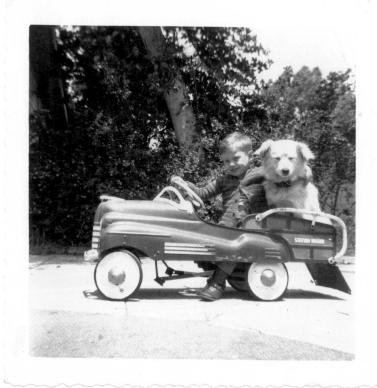

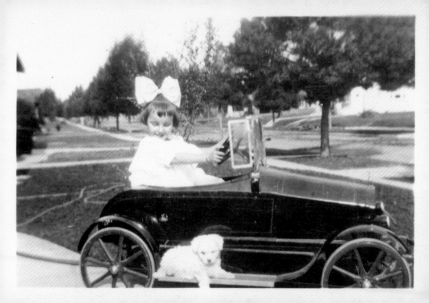

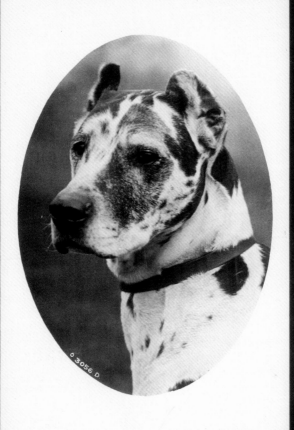

GREAT DANE

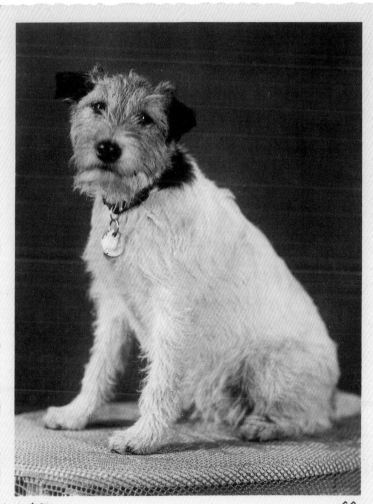

Fiffi

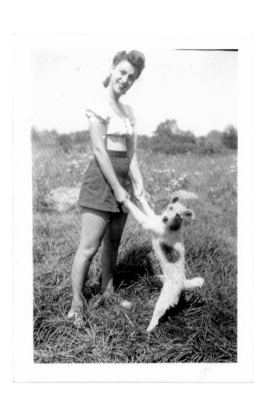
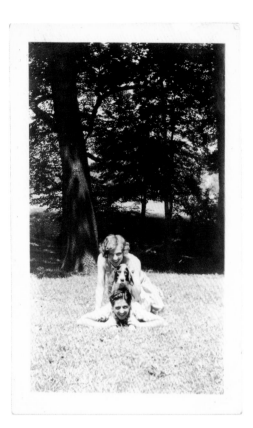
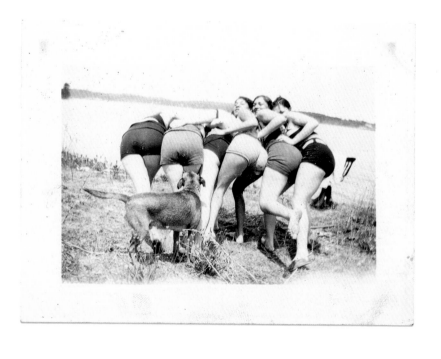

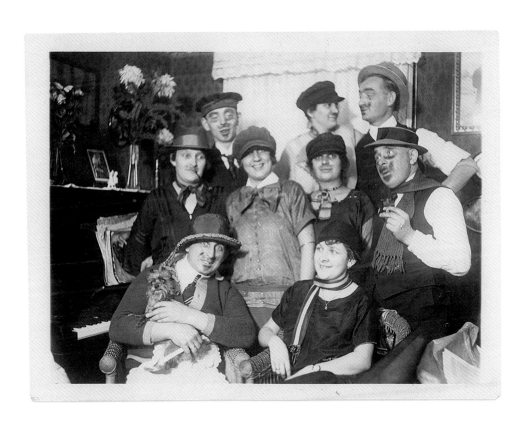

*I am convinced that basically
dogs think humans are nuts.
— John Steinbeck*

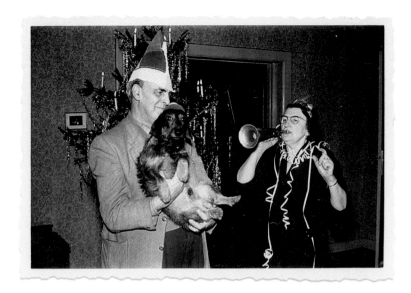

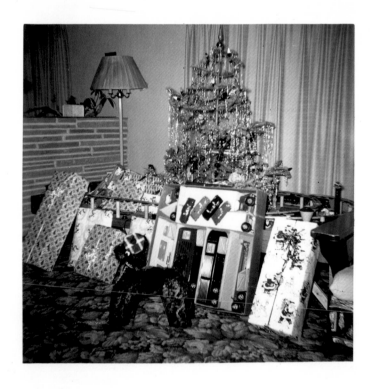

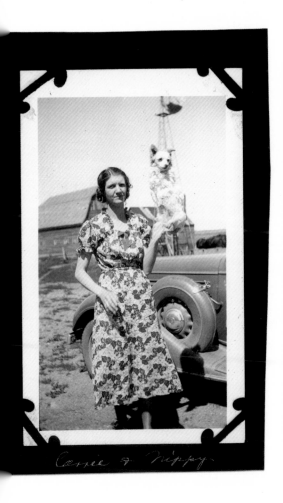

Carrie & Nippy

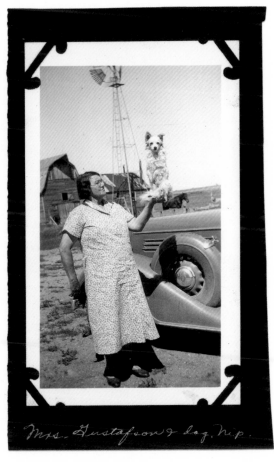

Mrs. Gustafson & dog, Nip.

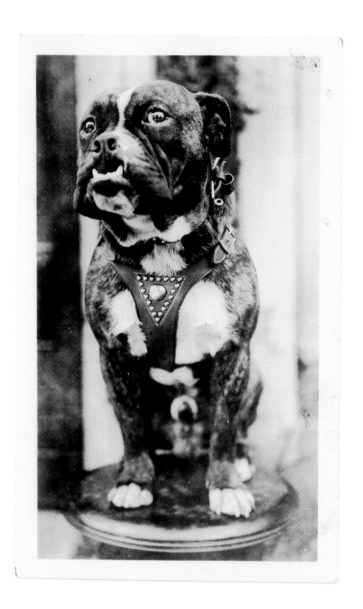

*You do not own a dog;*
*the dog owns you.*
*— Anonymous*

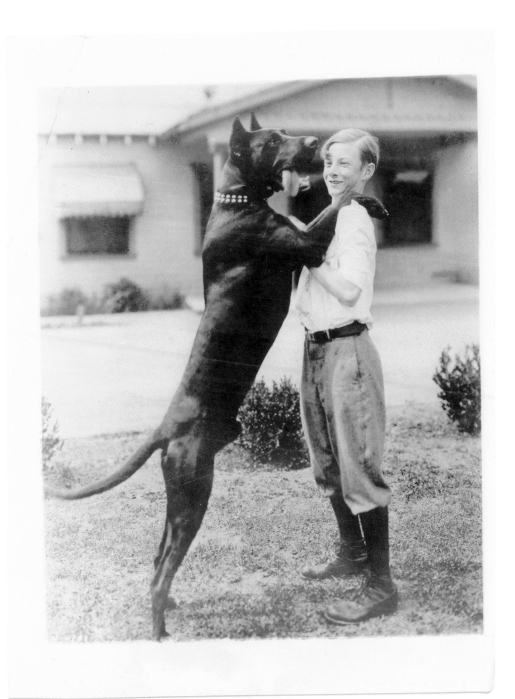

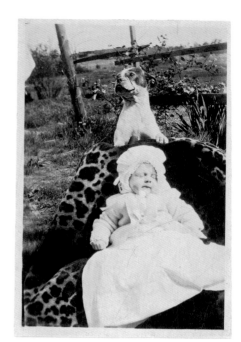

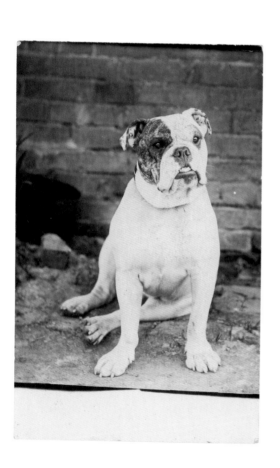

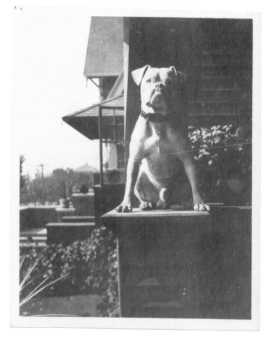

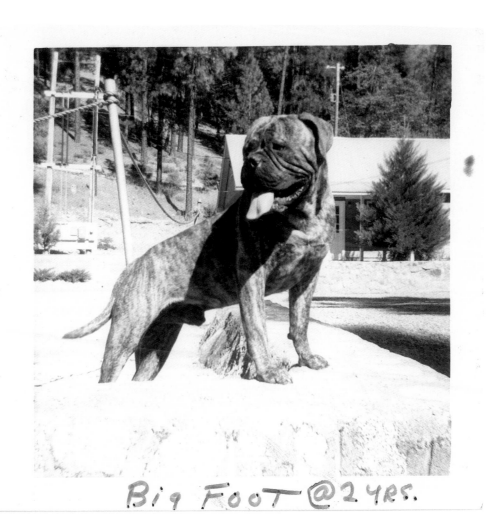

Big Foot @ 2 yrs.

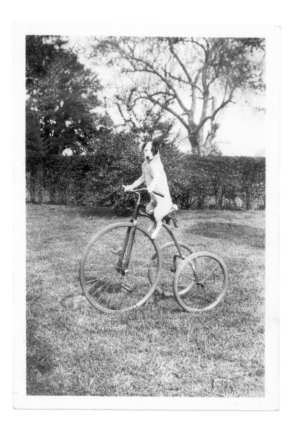

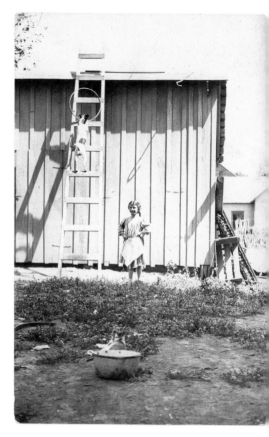

*There is only one smartest dog
in the world, and everybody has it.
— Anonymous*

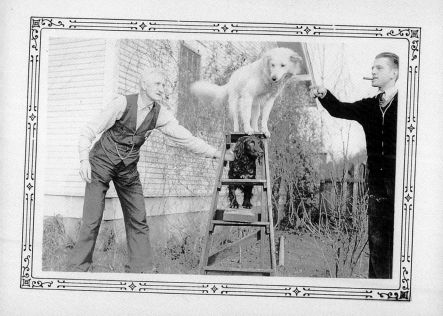

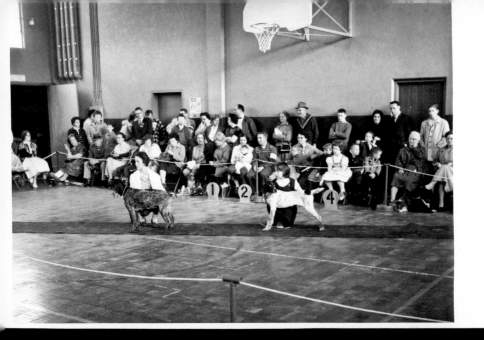

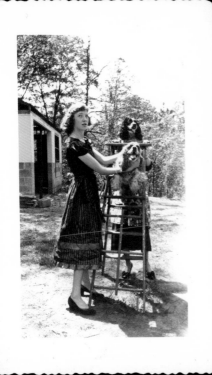

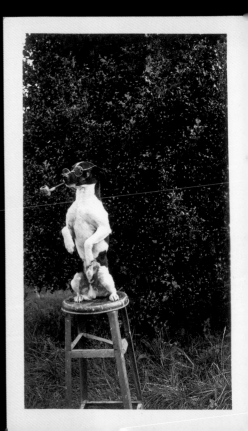

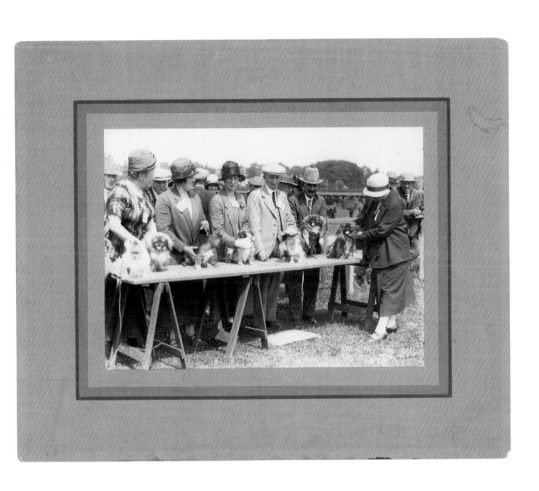

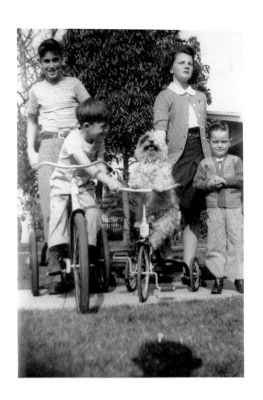

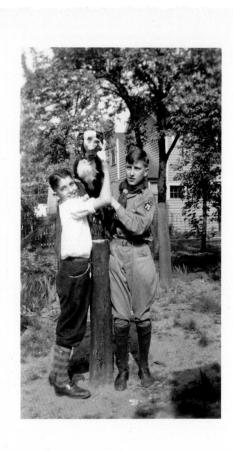

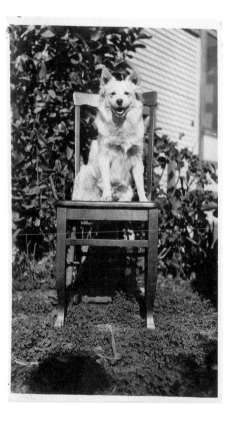

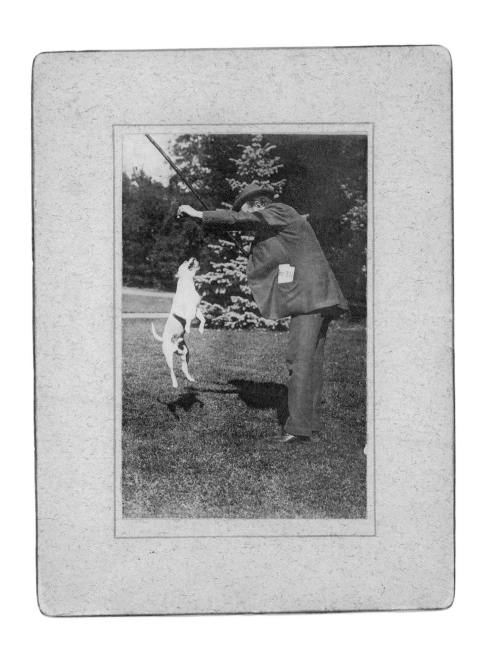

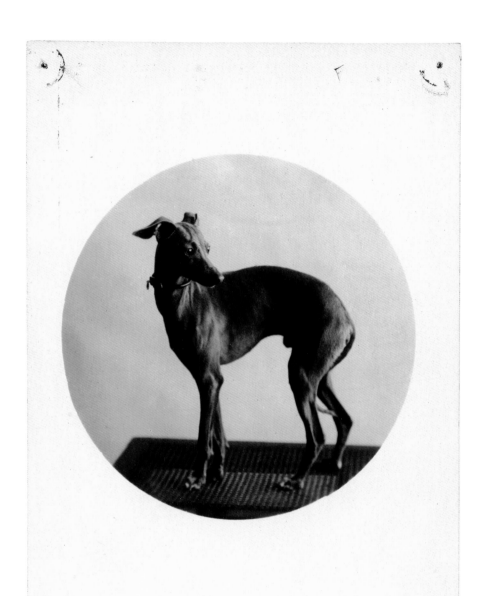

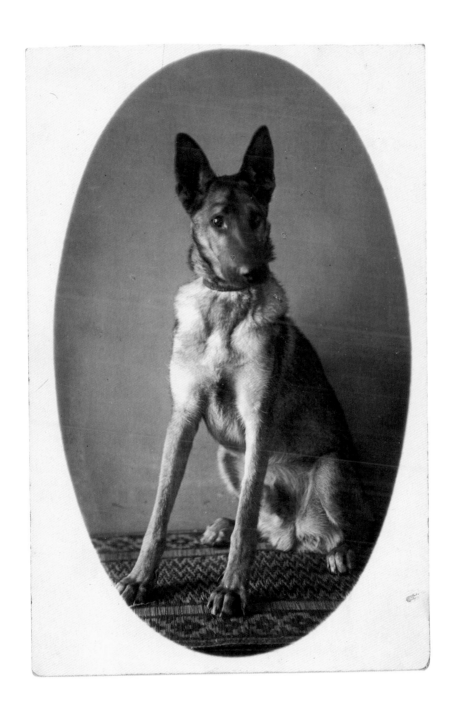

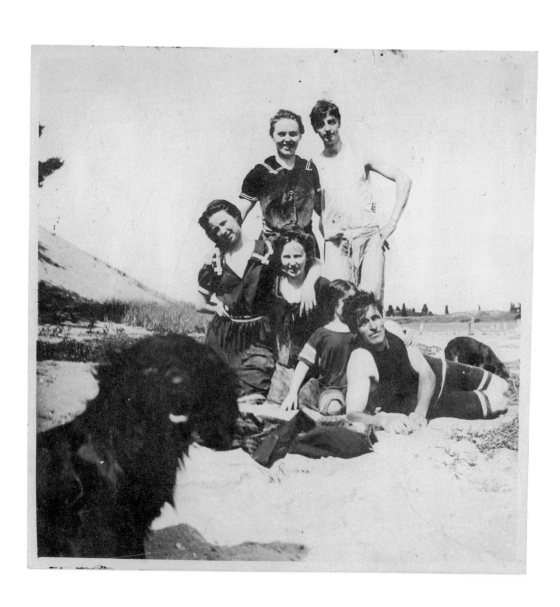

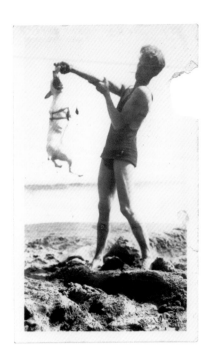

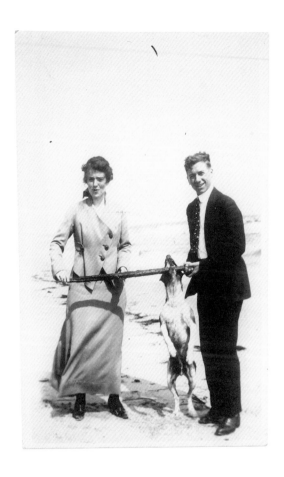

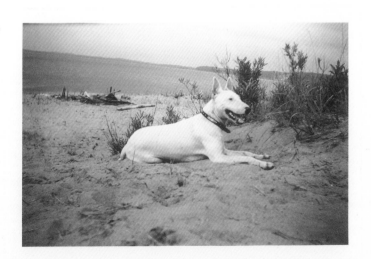

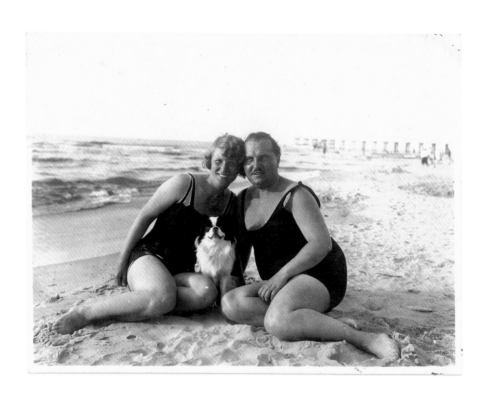

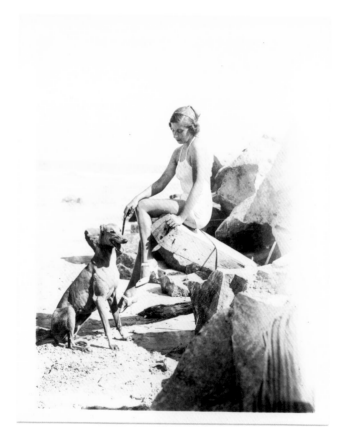

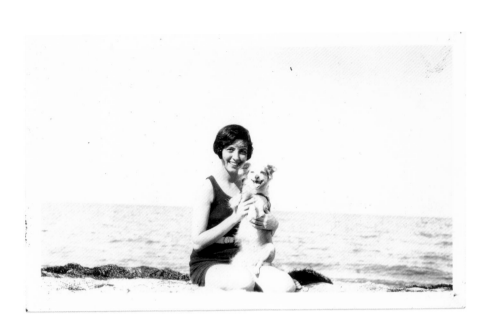

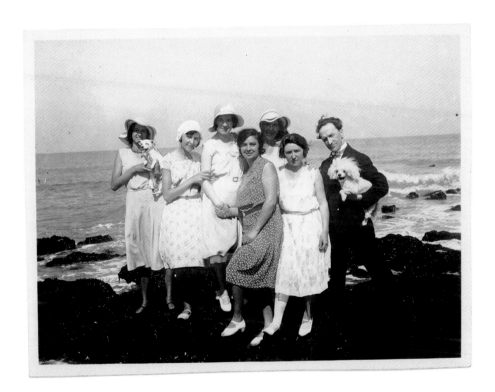

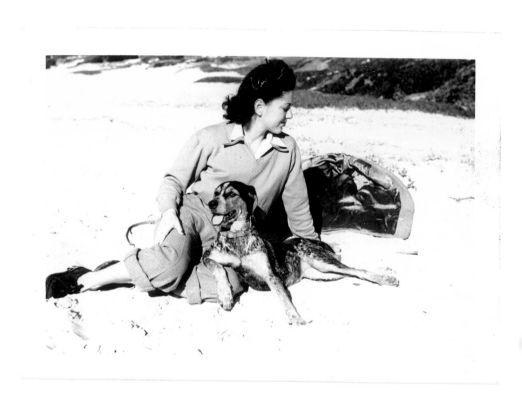

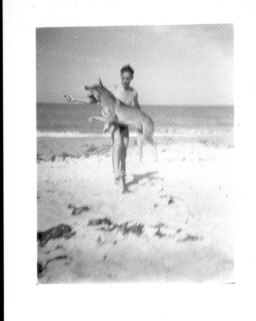
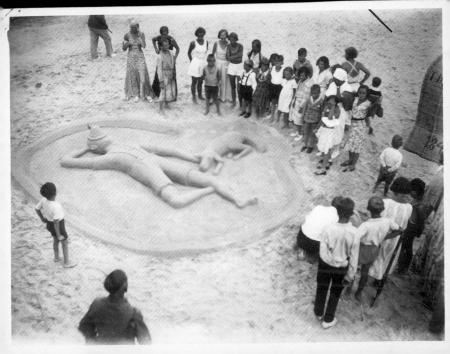

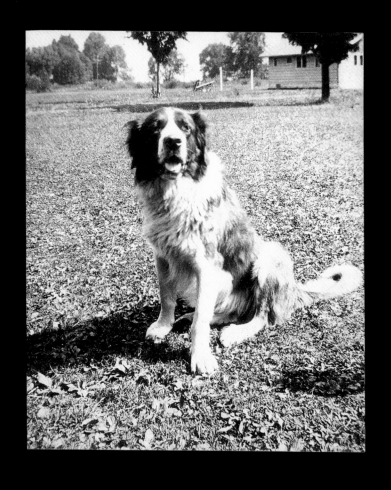

Rambunctious, rumbustious,
delinquent dogs become angelic
when sitting.
— Dr. Ian Dunbar

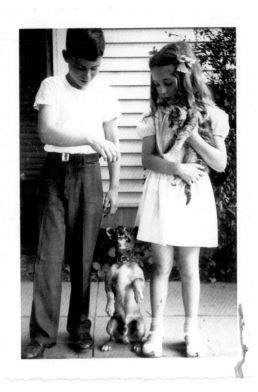

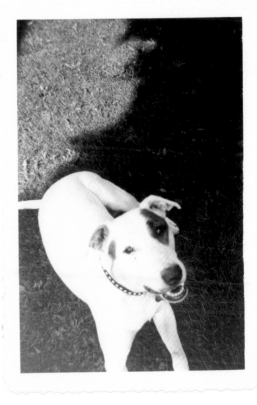

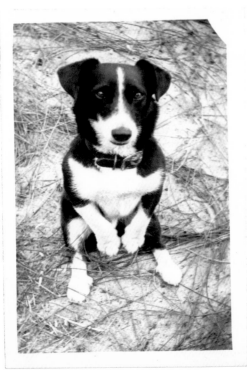

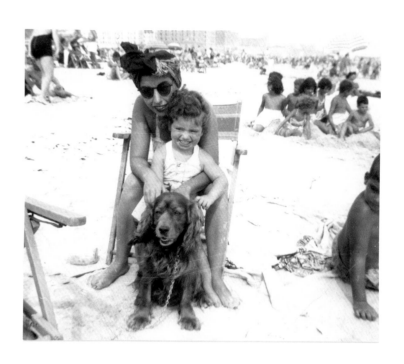

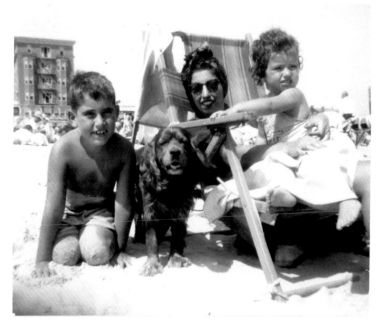

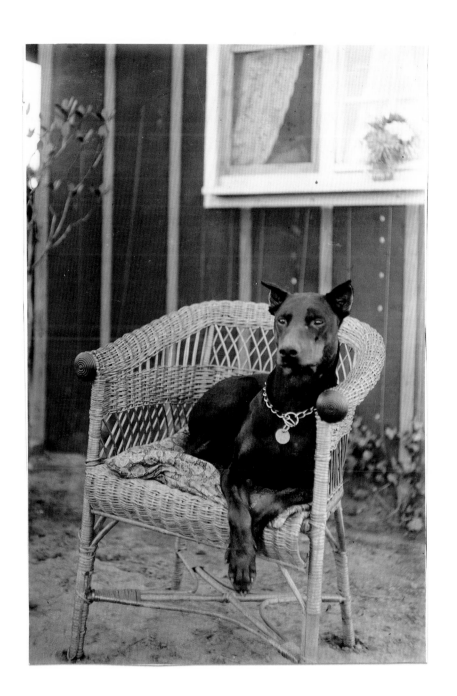

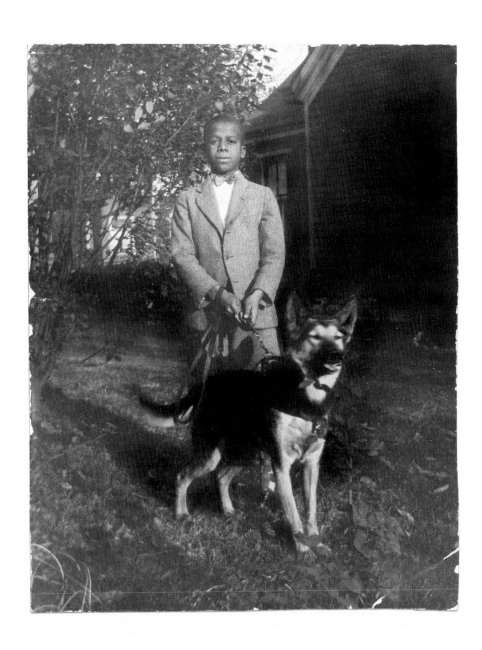

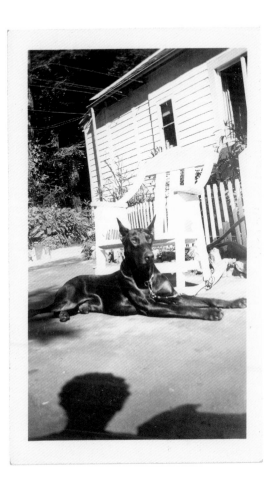
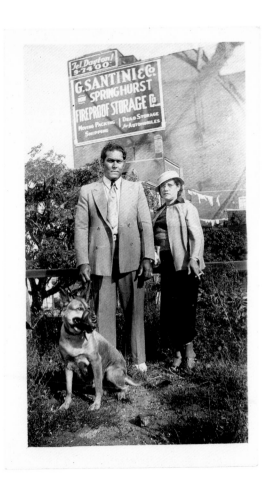

*You always sympathize
with the underdog unless the
other dog is yours.
— Anonymous*

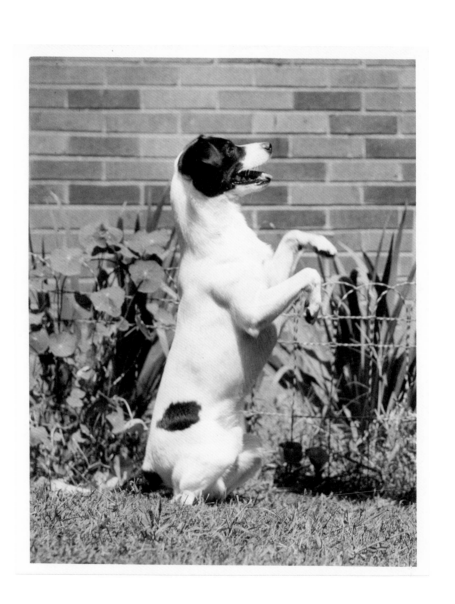

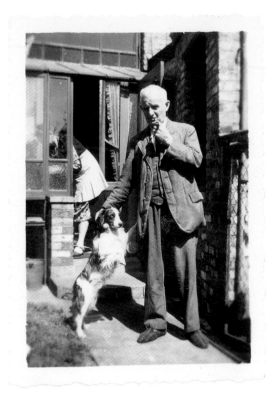

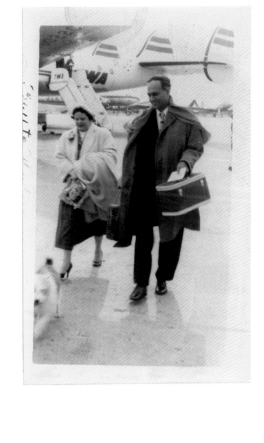

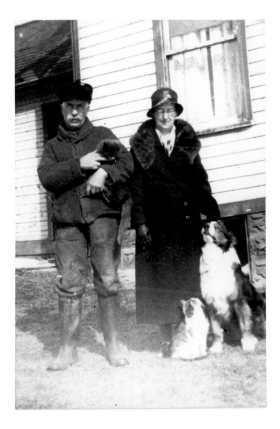

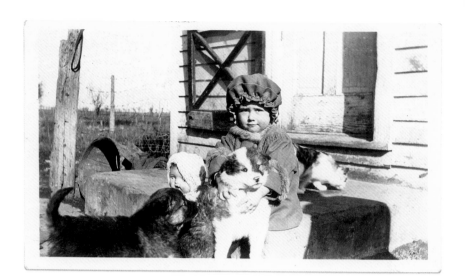

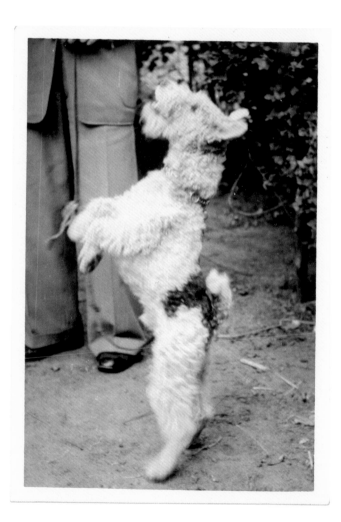

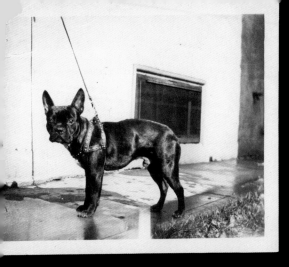

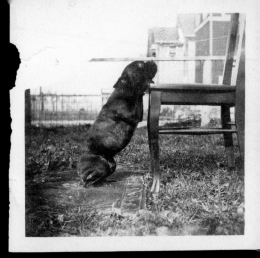

*Most dogs don't think
they are human; they know they are.*
*— Jane Swann*

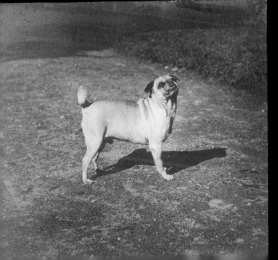

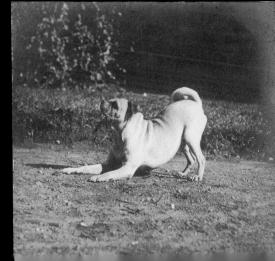

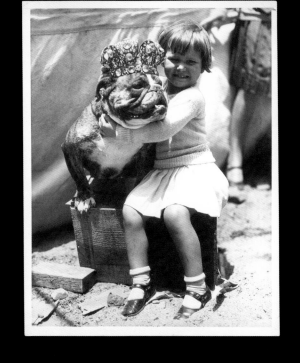

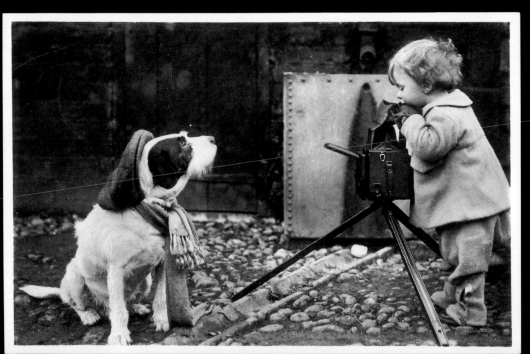

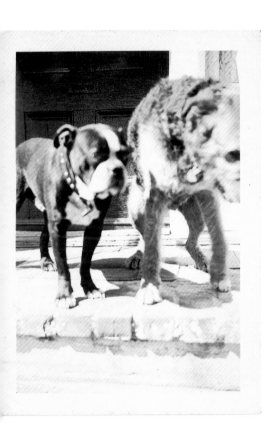
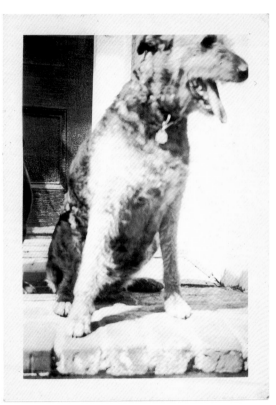

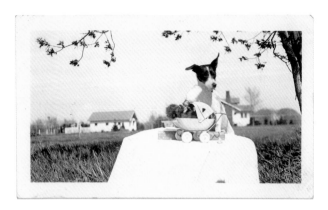

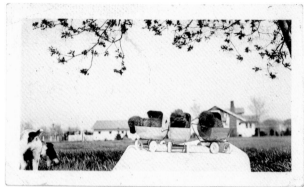

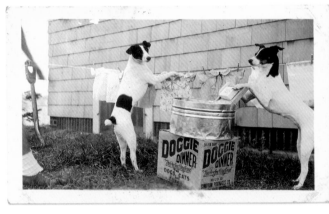

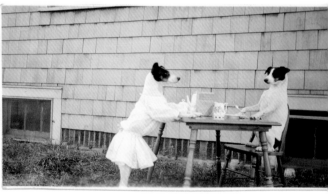

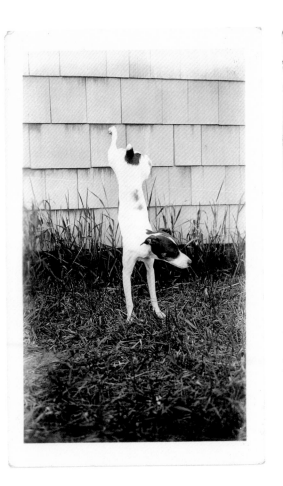
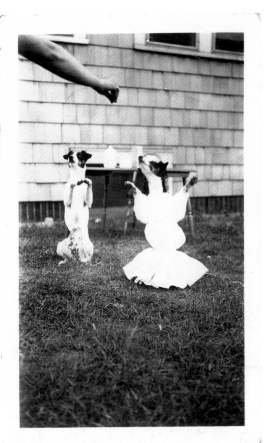

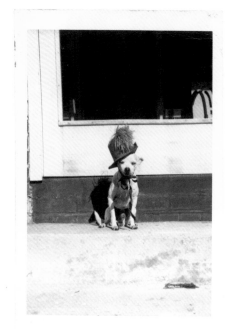

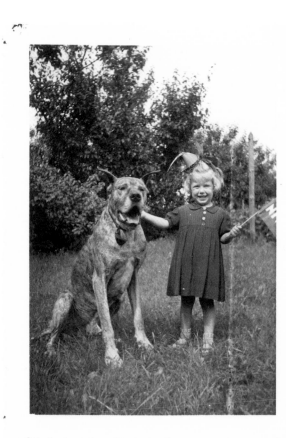

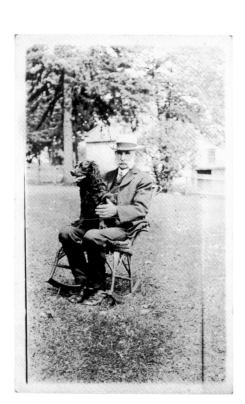

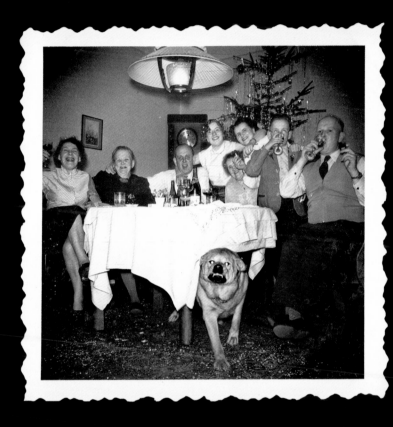

*Every dog is a lion at home.*
*— Giovanni Torriano*

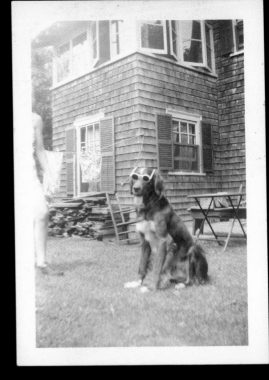

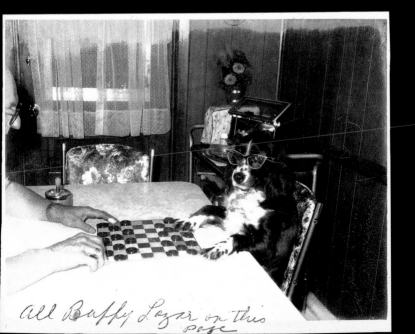

All Buffy Lazar on this page

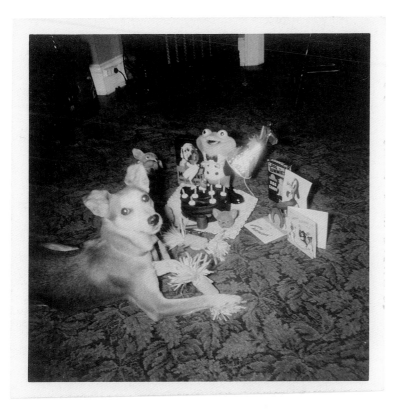
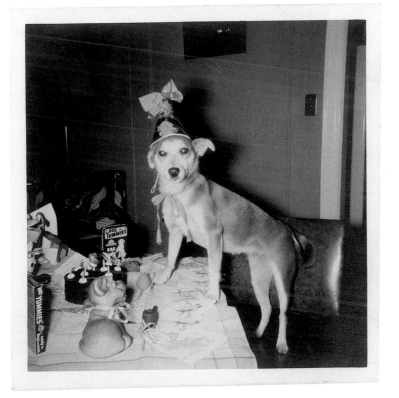

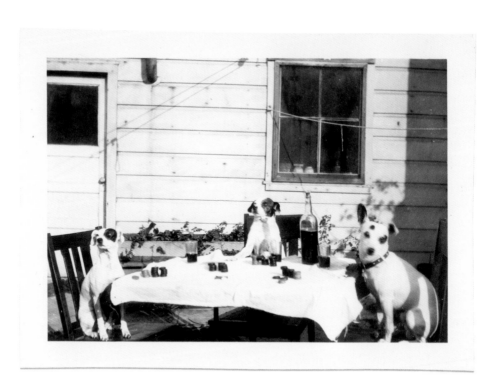

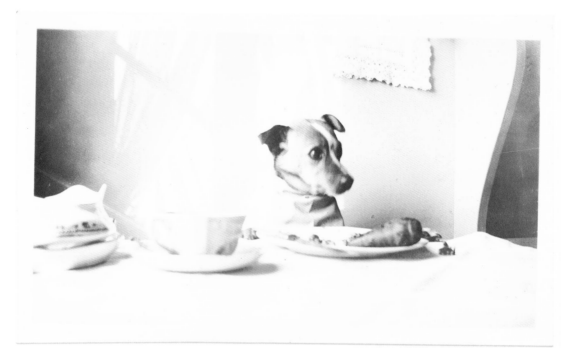

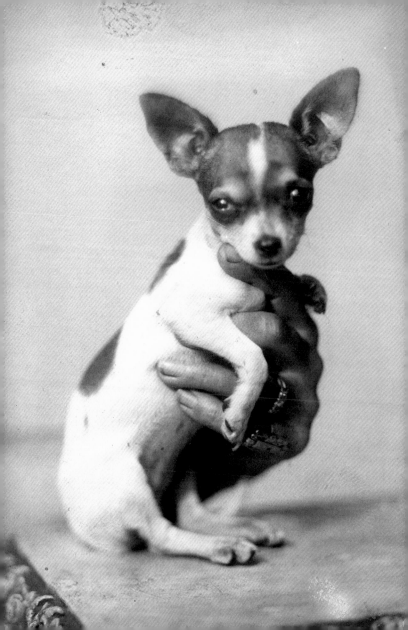

To call him a dog hardly seems to do him justice, though inasmuch as he has four legs, a tail, and barked, I admit he was to all outward appearances a dog. But to those of us who knew him well he was a perfect gentleman.
— Hermione Gingold

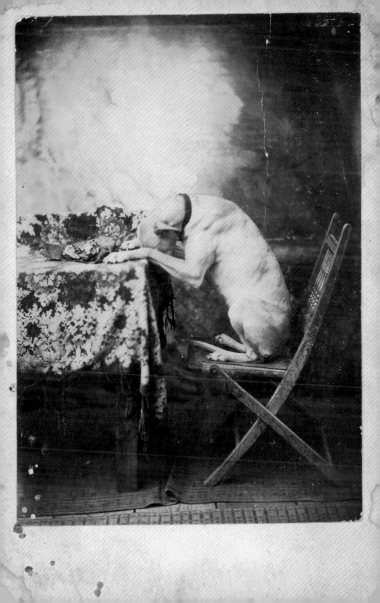

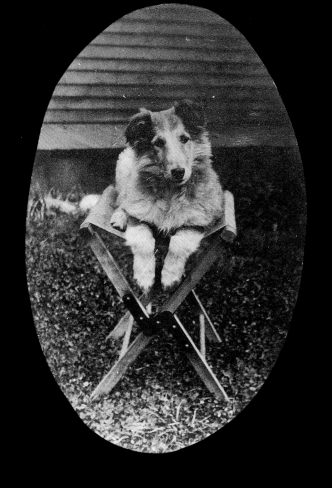

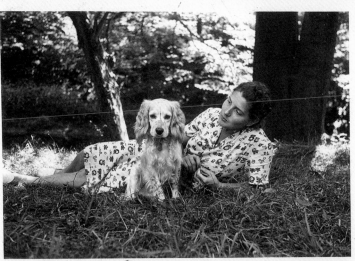

Taffy + Elsie — August 1940

"A man's best friend is his dog."

She passed away on May 19, 1941 at 8:30 pm. Just two weeks after this picture was taken.

She was born May 20, 1940 So she was one year and 2 3 days old

" Roll Over Chuckles " ...That's the girl " See You Laugh " 41 "

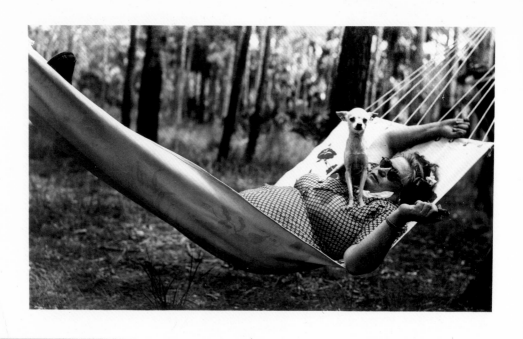

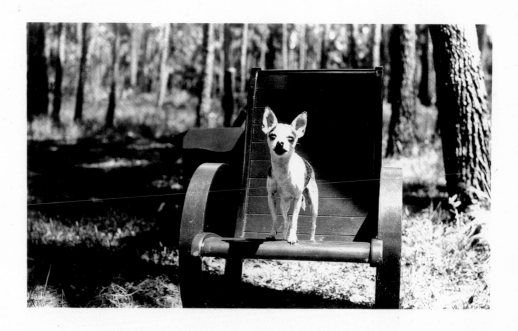

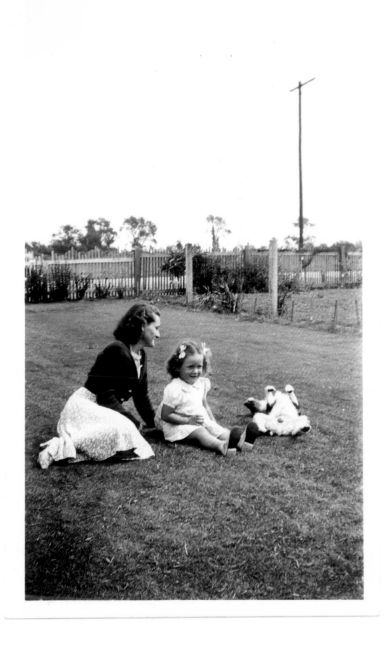

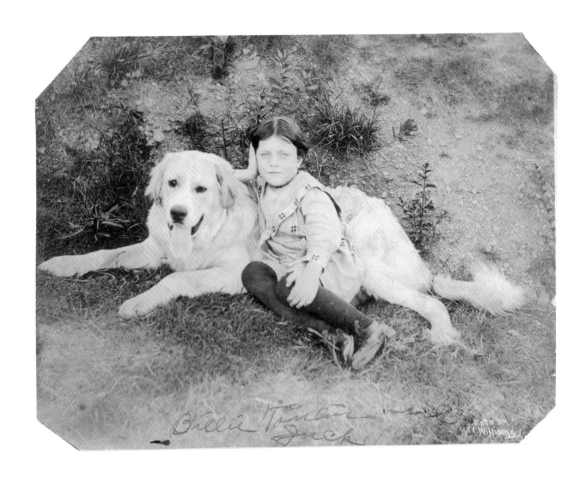

*If you don't own a dog, at least one, there is not necessarily anything wrong with you, but there may be something wrong with your life.*
— Roger Caras

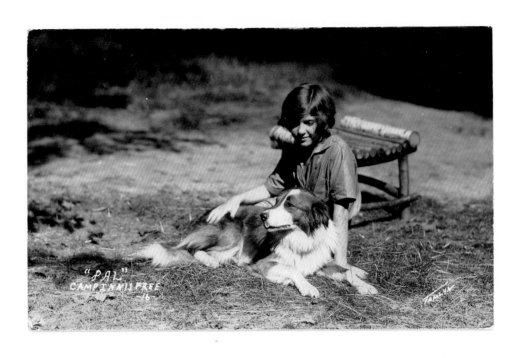

"PAL"
CAMP TANISFREE
-16-

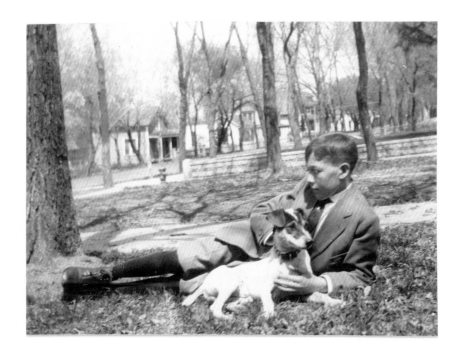

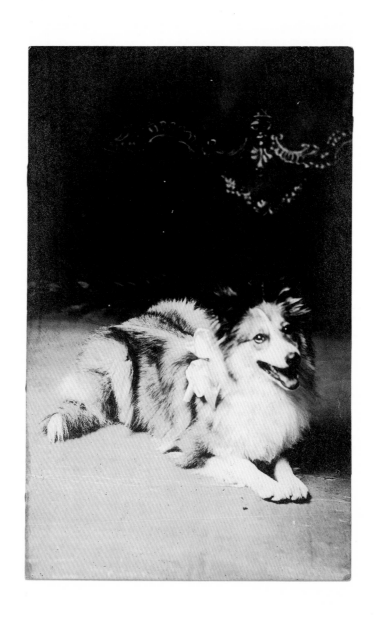

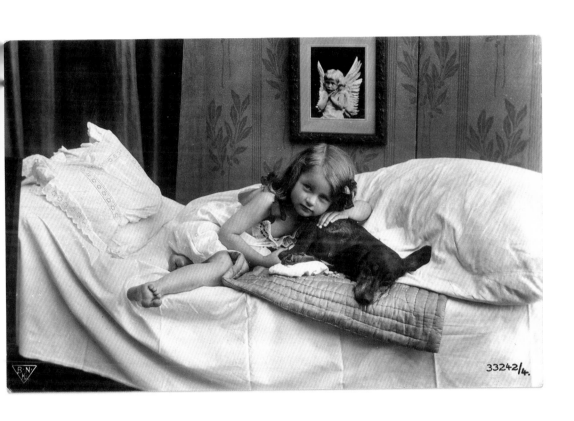

33242/4.

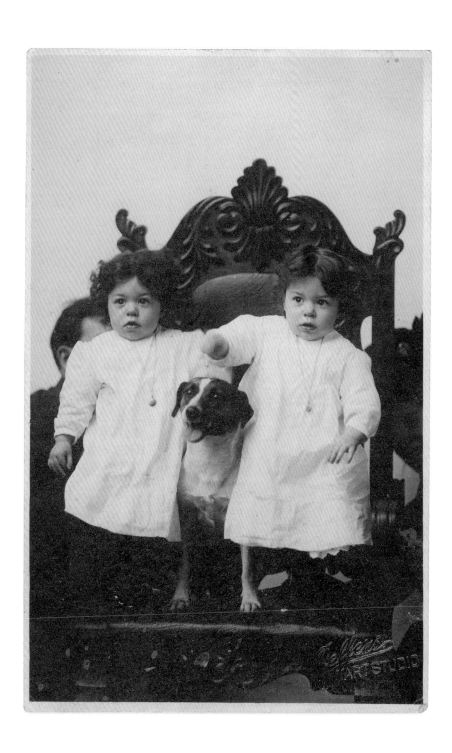

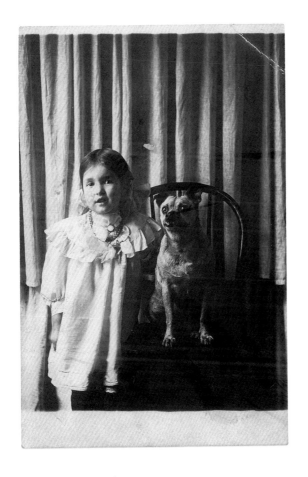
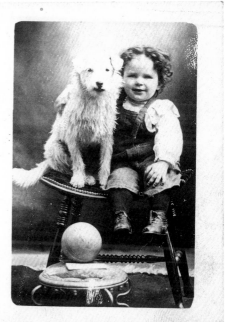

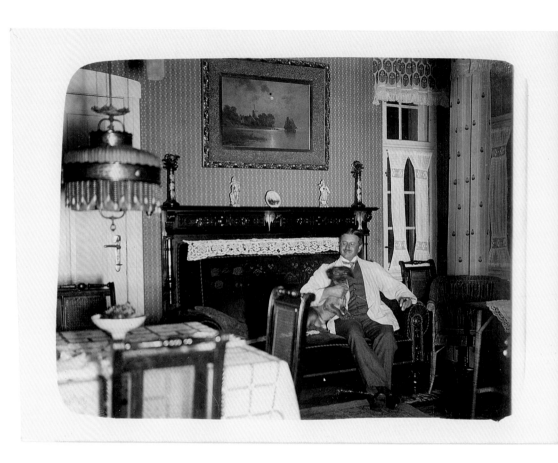

*If you want the best seat
in the house, move the dog.
— Anonymous*

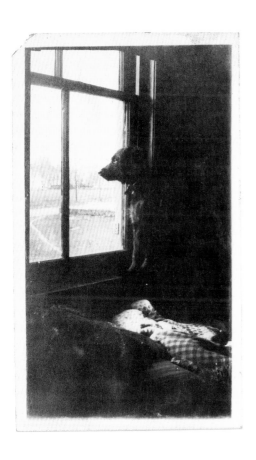

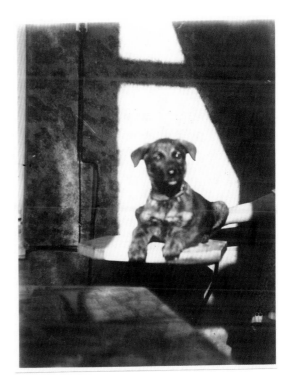

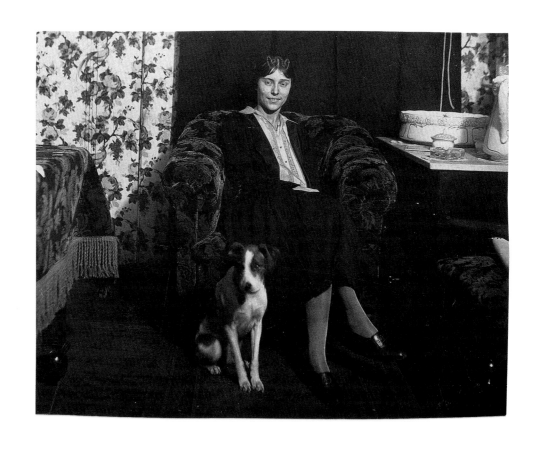

*Animals are such agreeable friends —*
*they ask no questions,*
*they pass no criticisms.*
*— George Eliot*

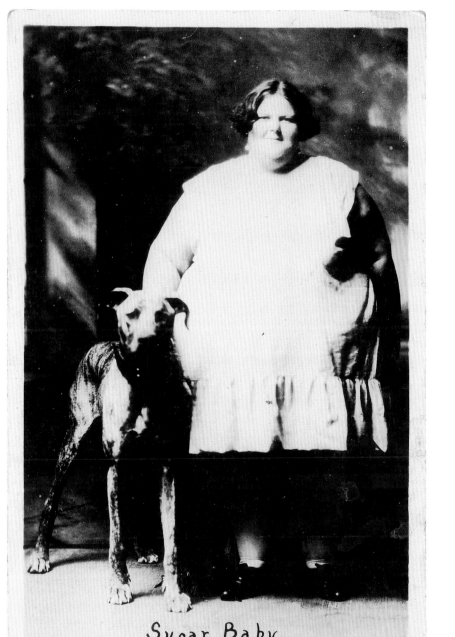

Sugar Baby

500 lbs — Age 18

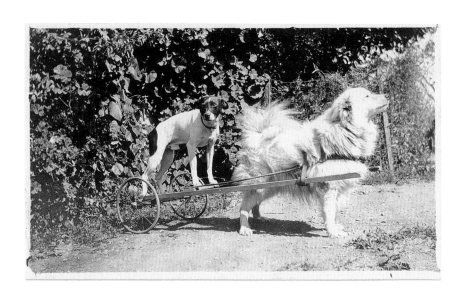

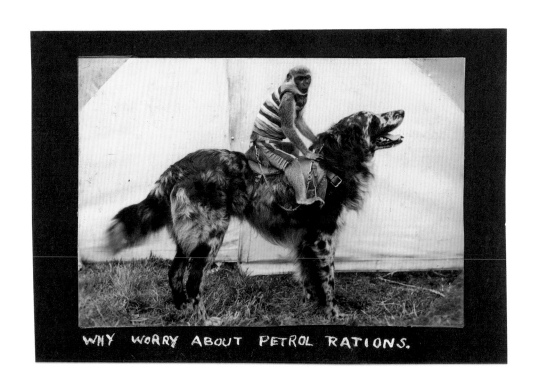

WHY WORRY ABOUT PETROL RATIONS.

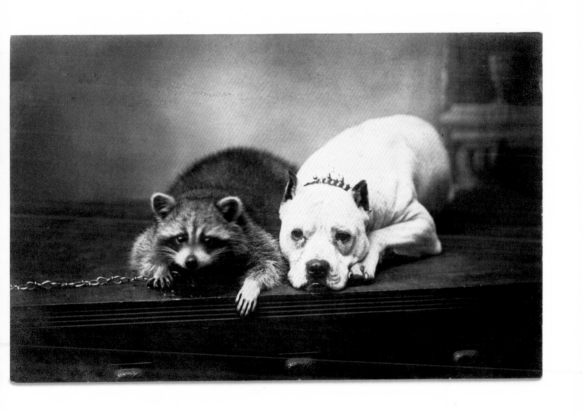

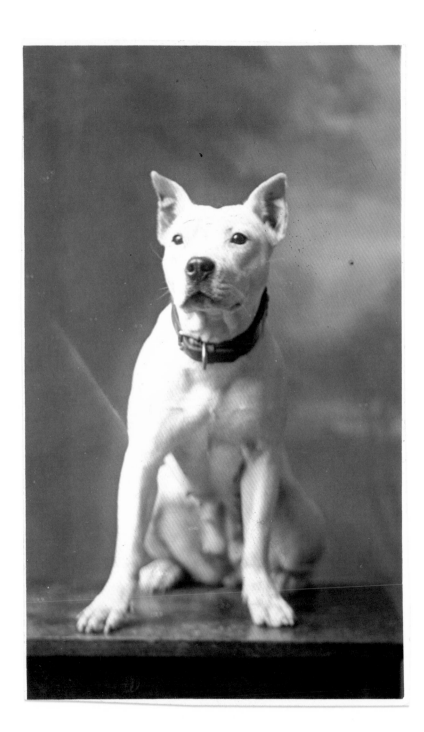

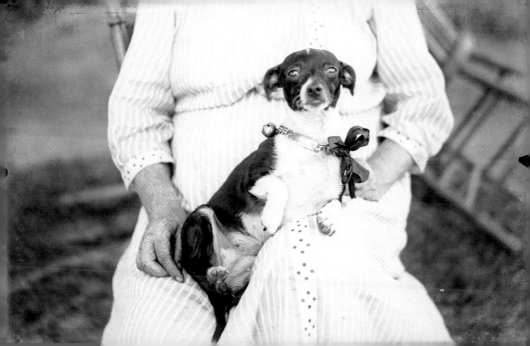

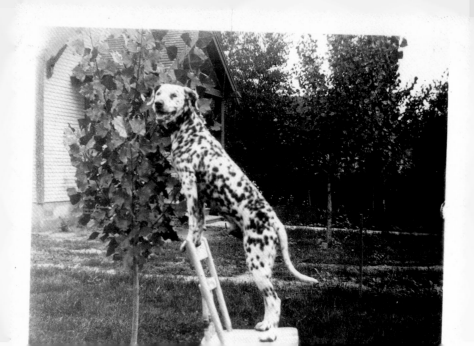

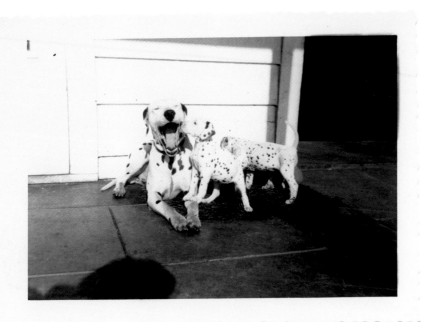

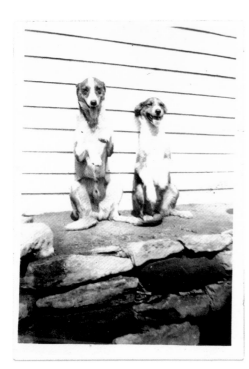

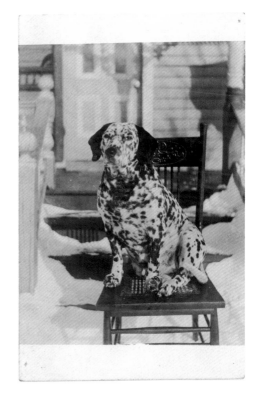

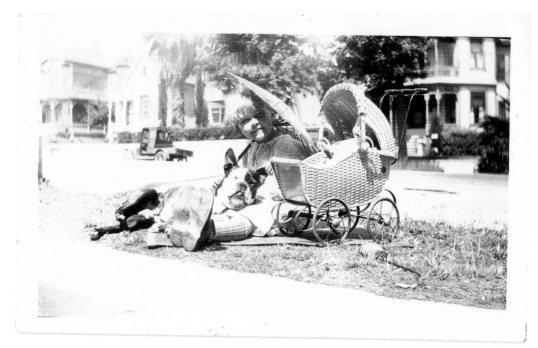

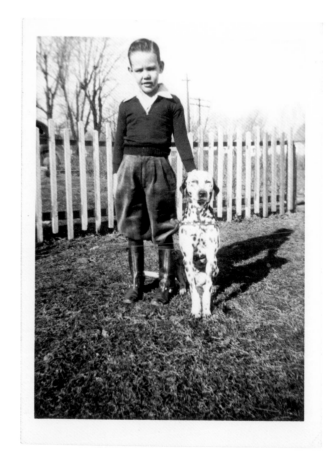

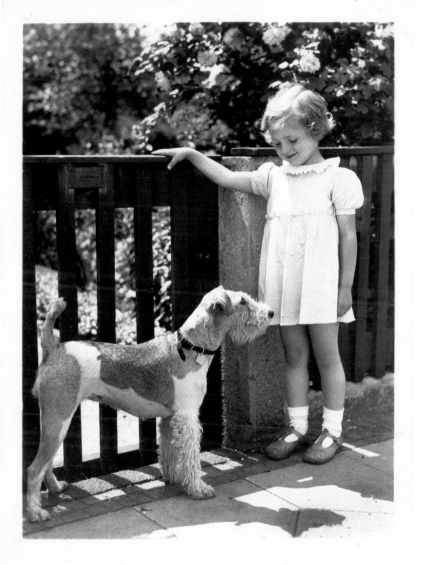

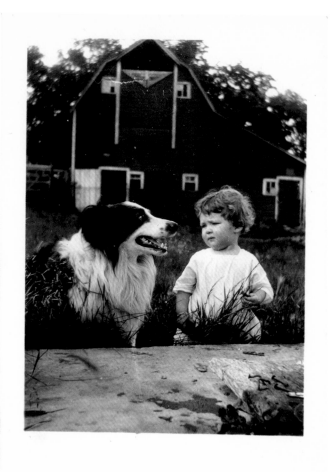

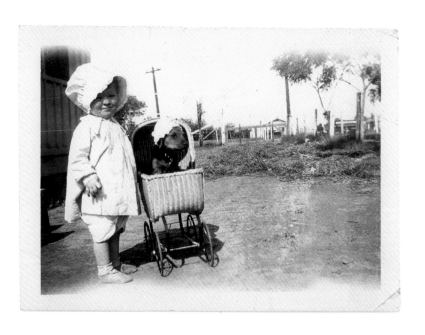

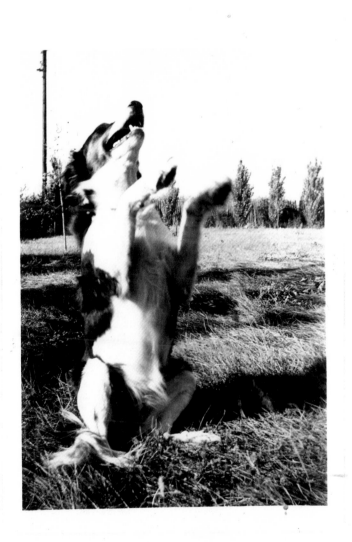

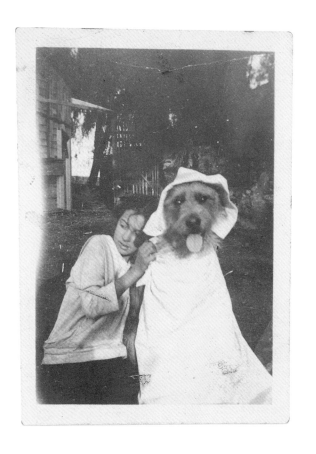
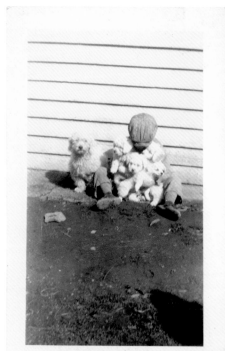
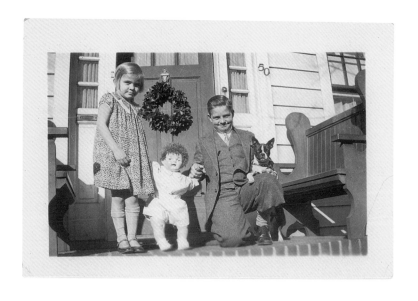

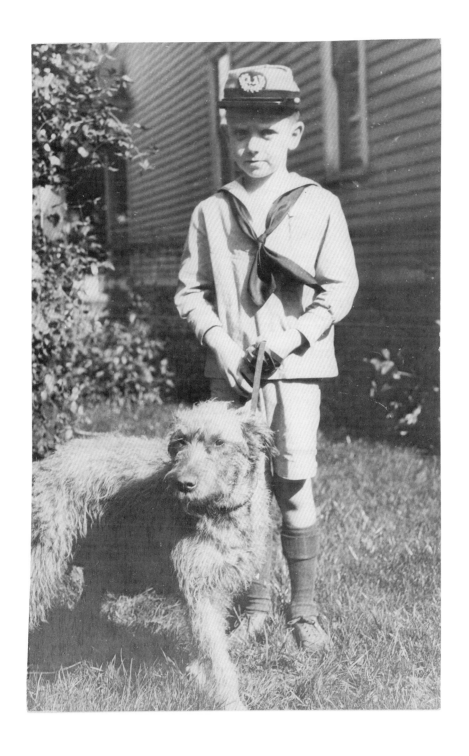

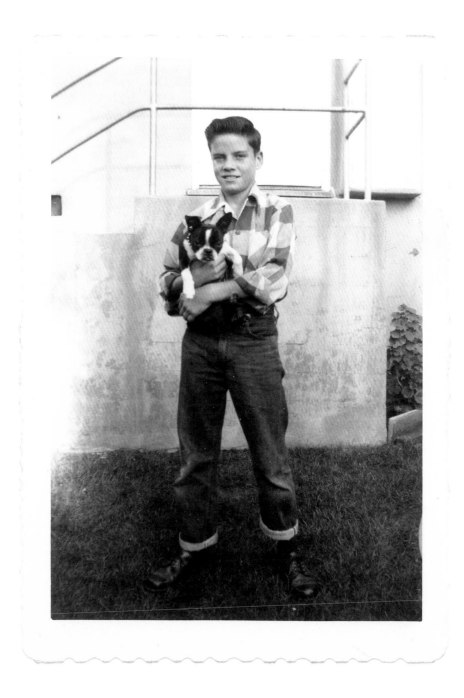

*Real men love little dogs too.*
*— Catherine Johnson*

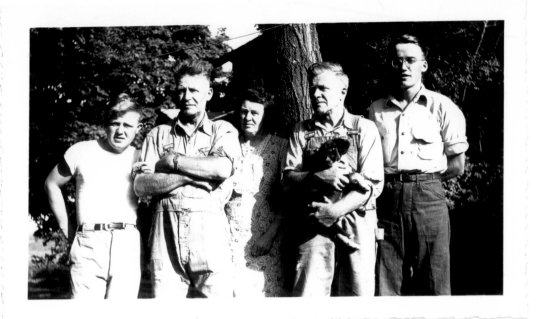

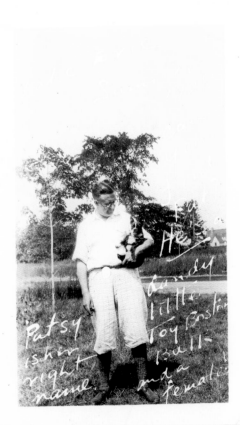

Patsy
is his
right
name

He

andy
little
Toy Boston
bull
and a
female

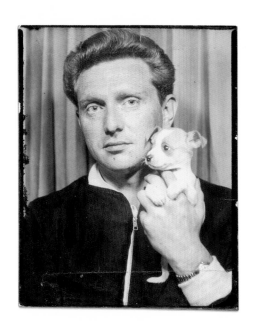

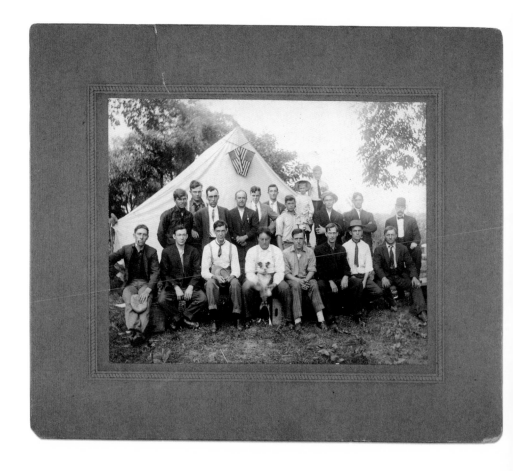

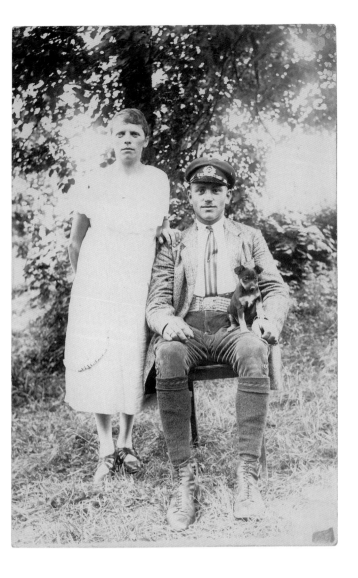

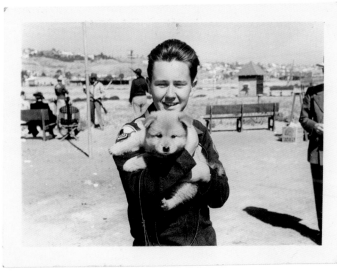

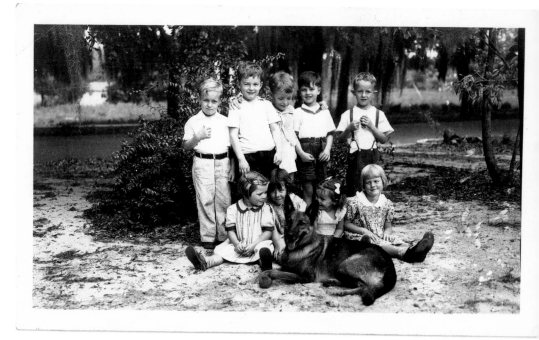

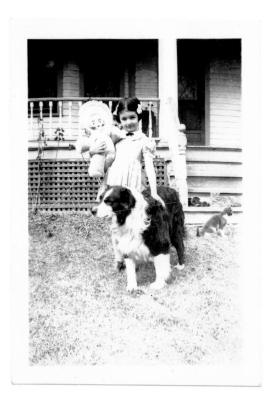

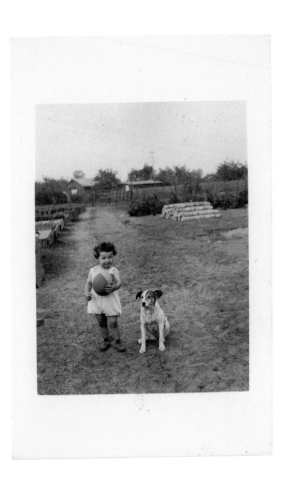

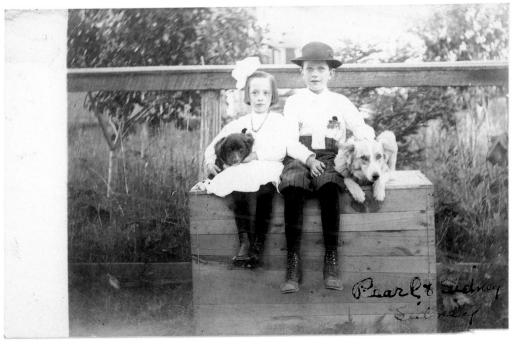

Pearl & Sidney
Sidney

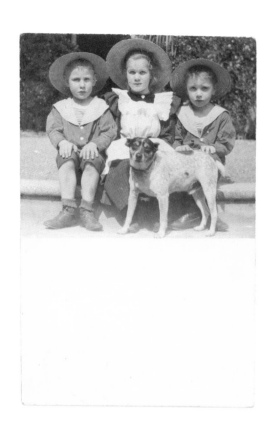
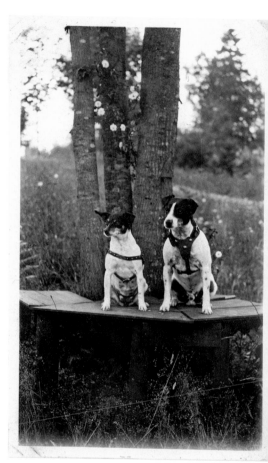

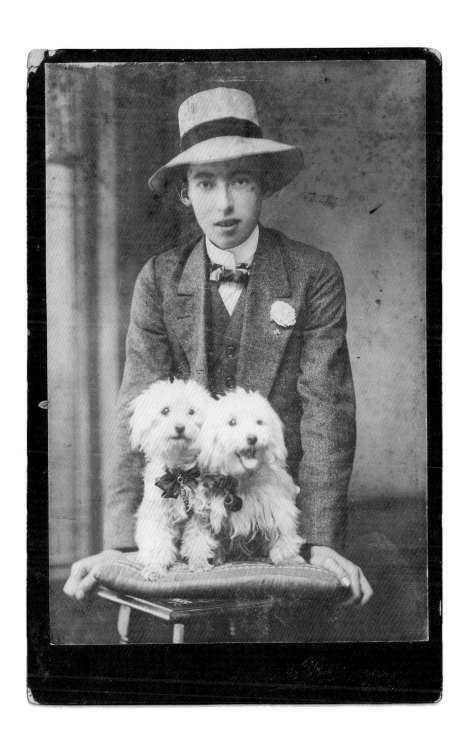

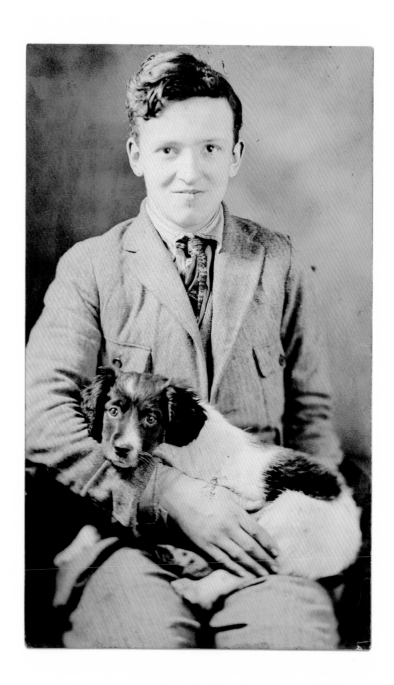

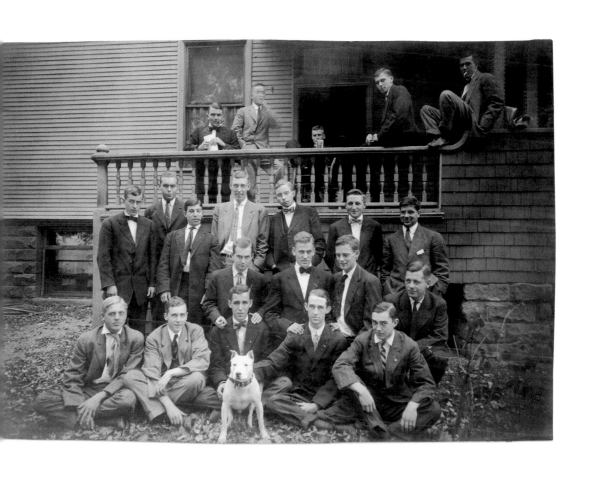

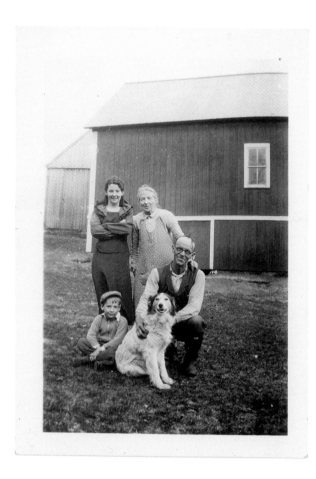

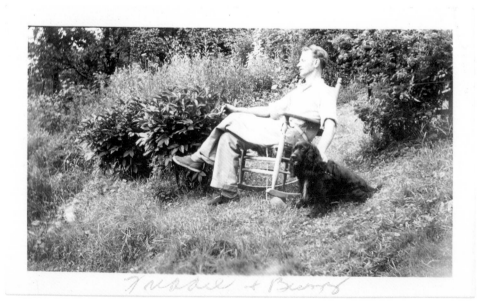

*Arnold & Berry*

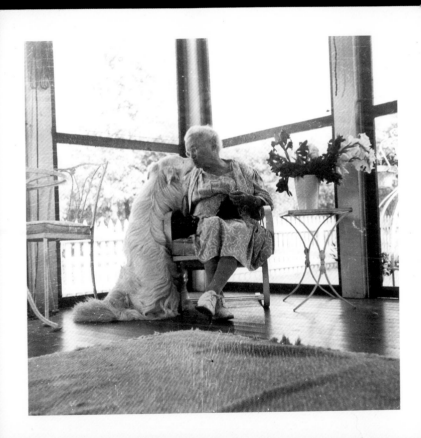

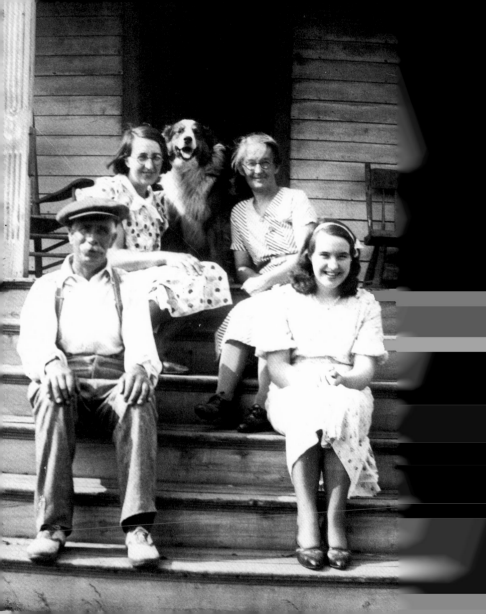

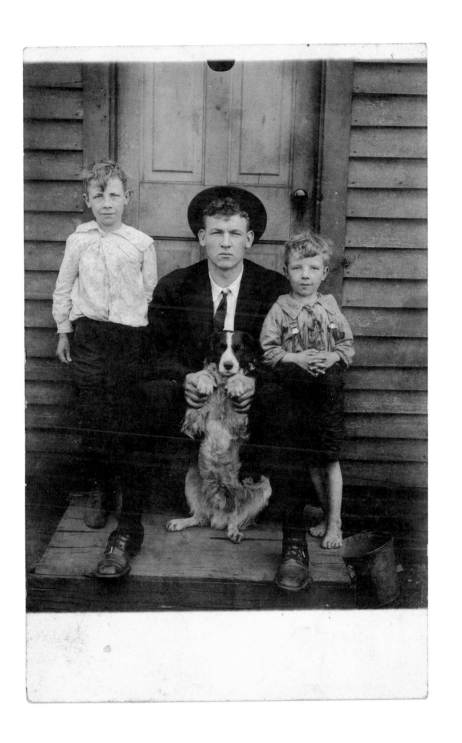

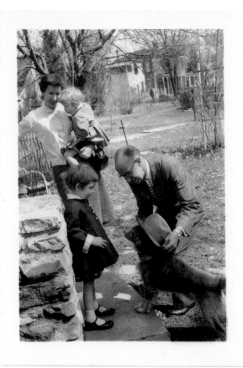

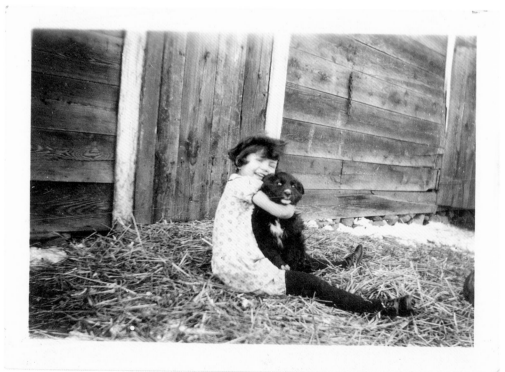

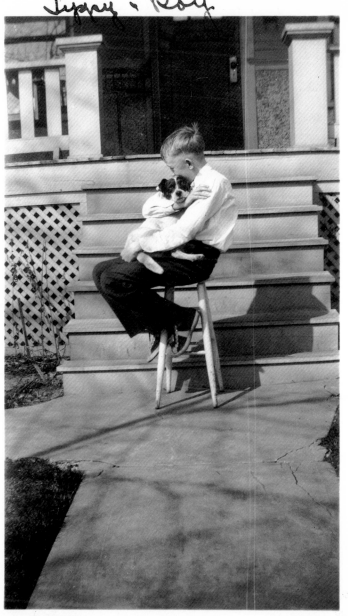

Tippy & Roy

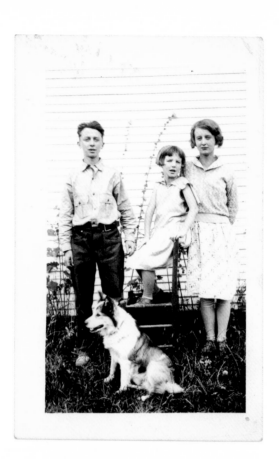

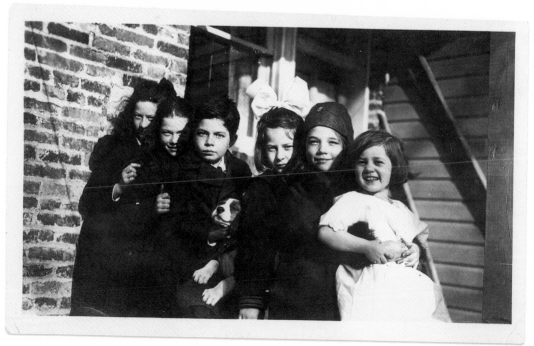

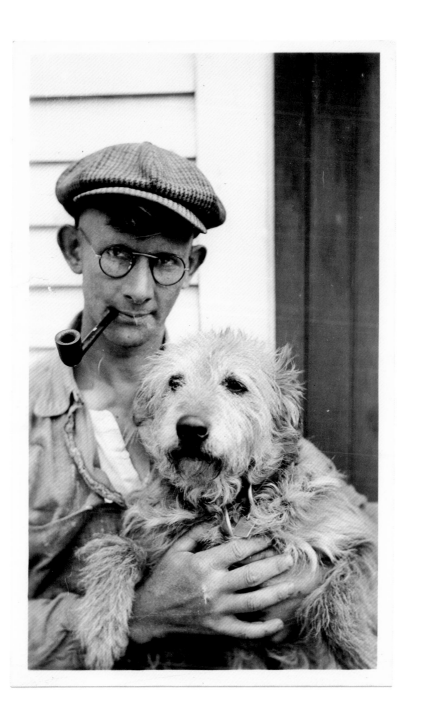

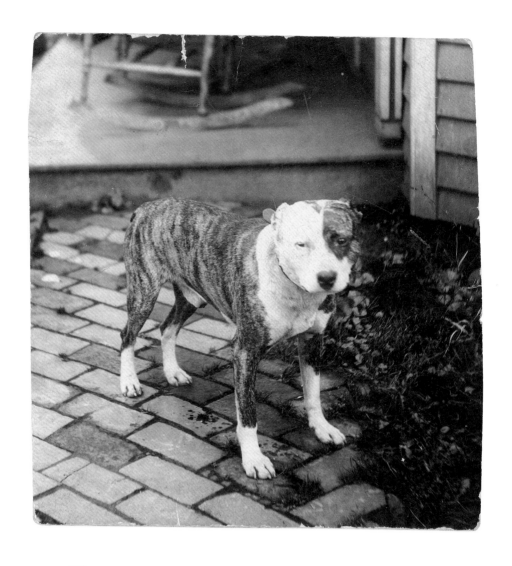

Dogs are our link to paradise.
They don't know evil or jealousy
or discontent.
— Milan Kundera

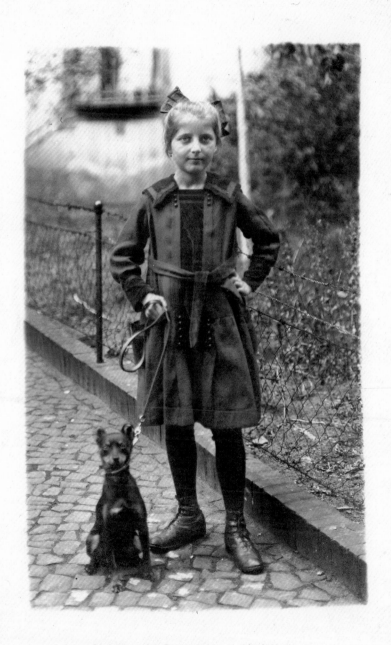

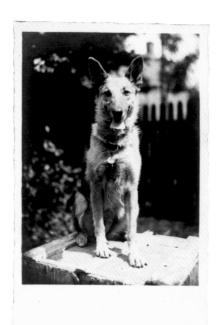

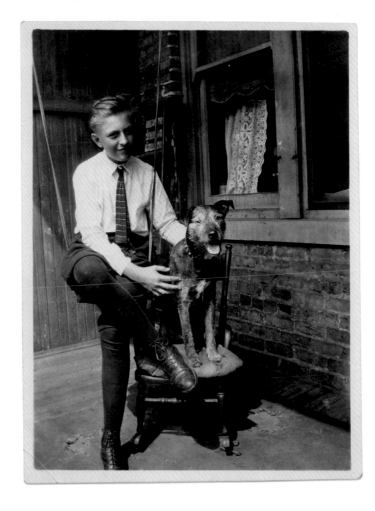

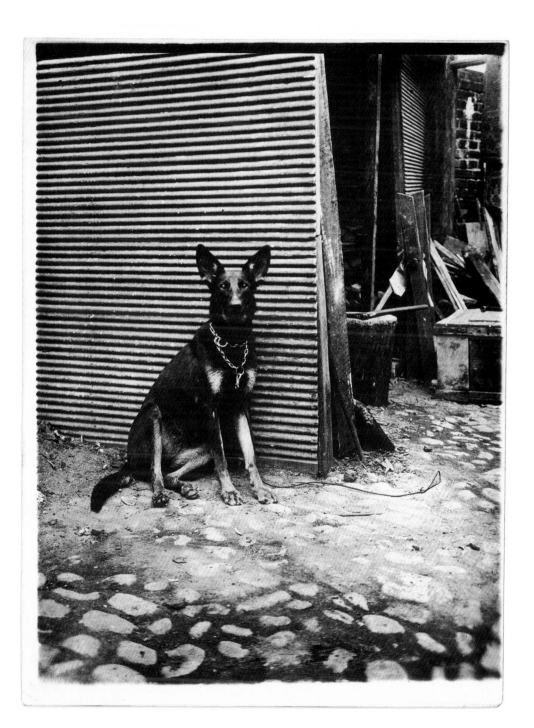

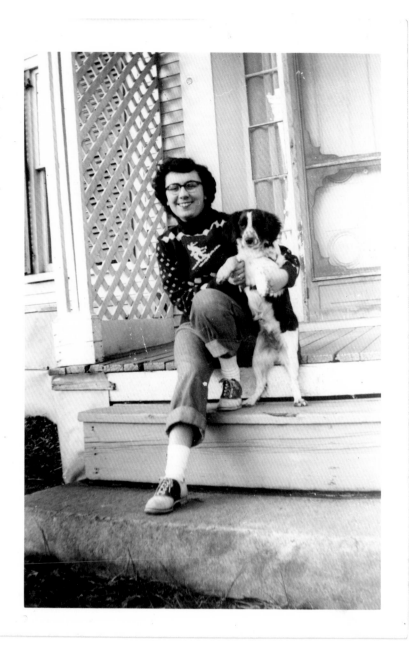

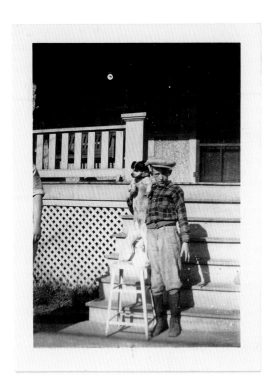

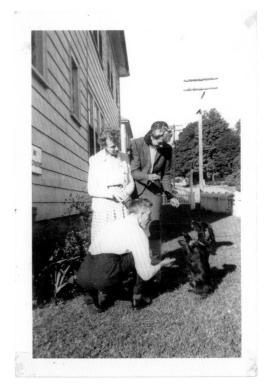

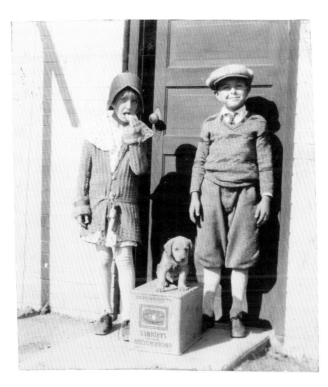

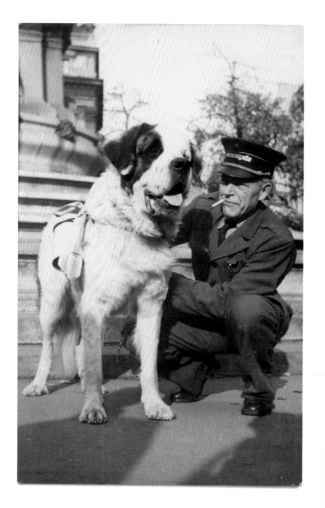

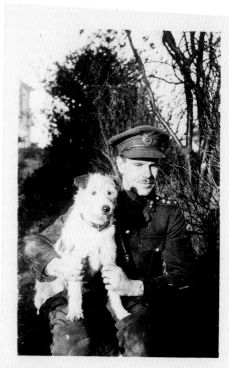

*In order to really enjoy a dog,
one doesn't merely try to train him
to be semi-human. The point of it
is to open oneself to the possibility of
becoming partly dog.*
*— Edward Hoagland*

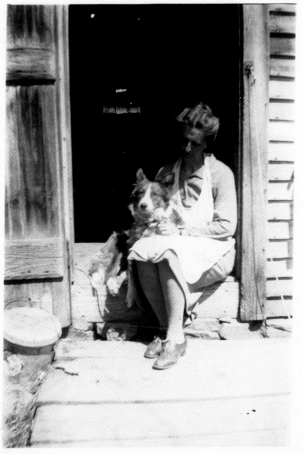

March 10 1934

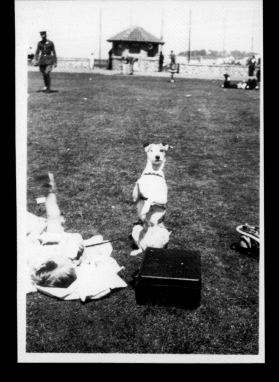
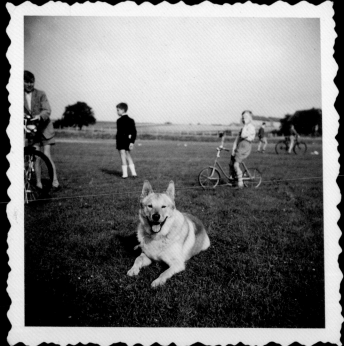

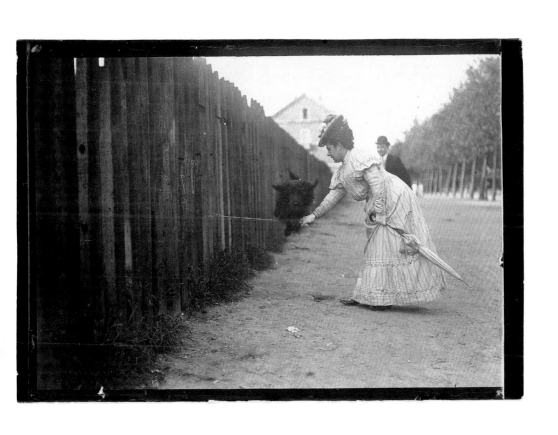

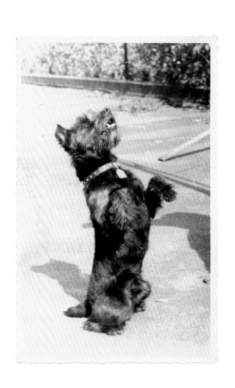

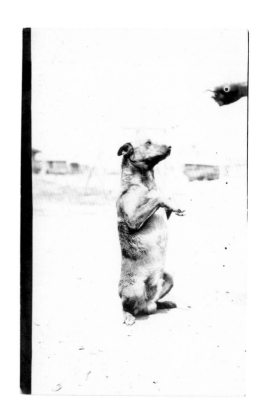

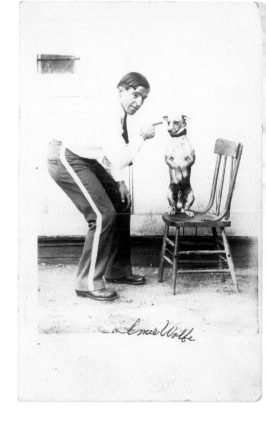

Emer Wolfe

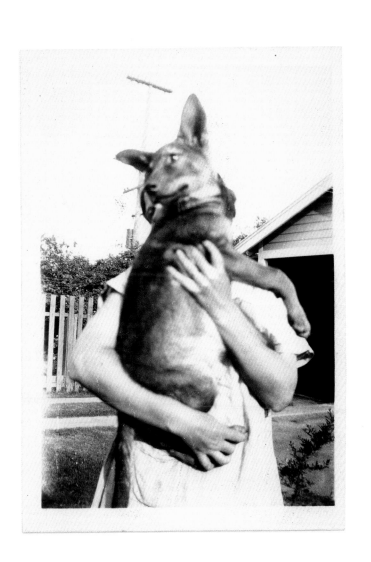

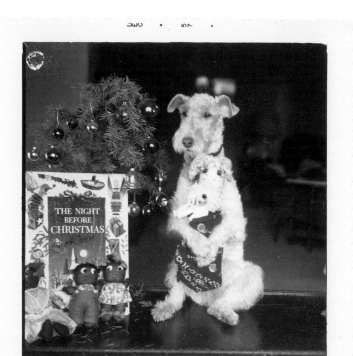

THE NIGHT
BEFORE
CHRISTMAS

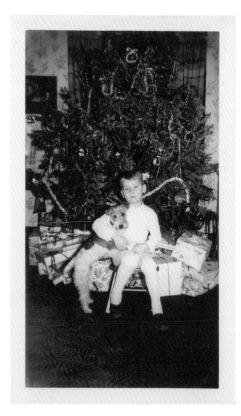

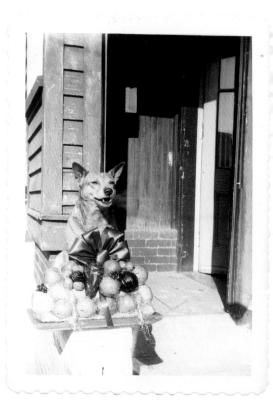

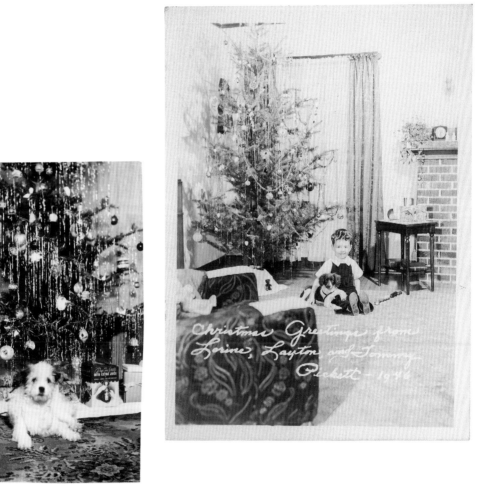

Christmas Greetings from
Lorine, Layton and Tommy
Pickett - 1946

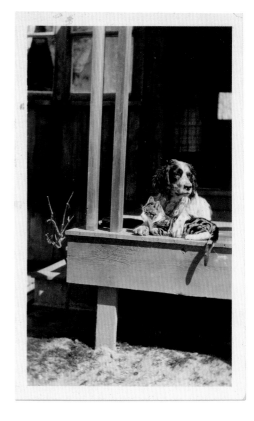

To err is human,
to forgive, canine.
— Anonymous

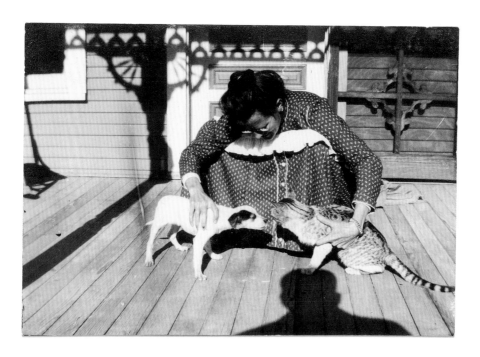

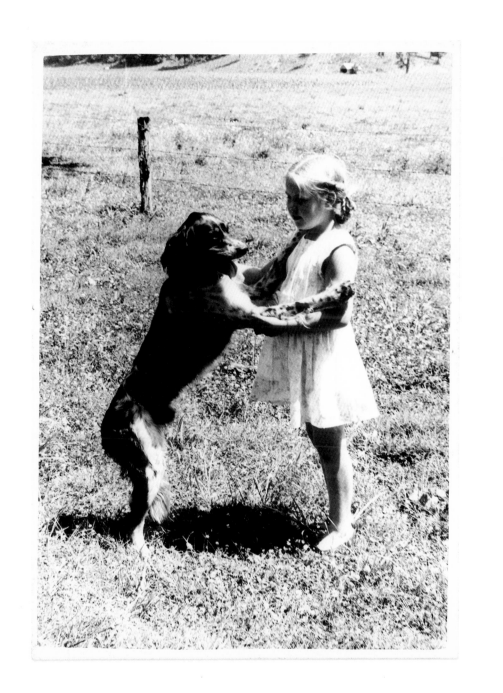

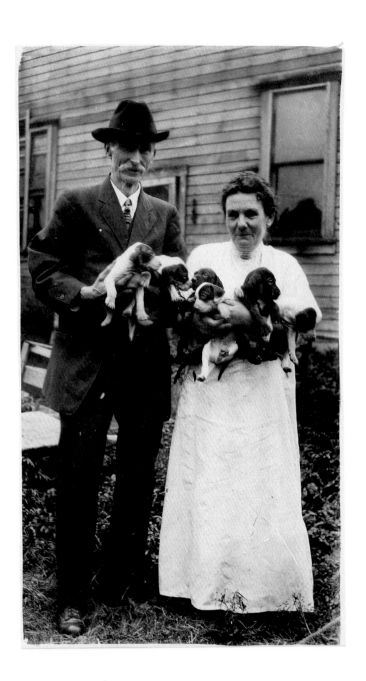

*No matter how little money and how few possessions you own, having a dog makes you rich.*
*— Louis Sabin*

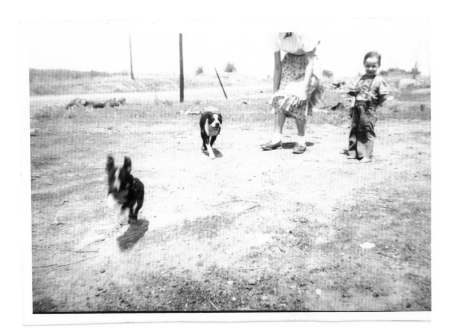

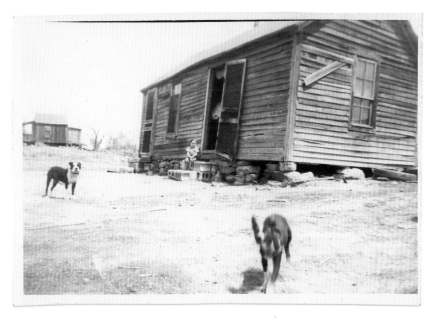

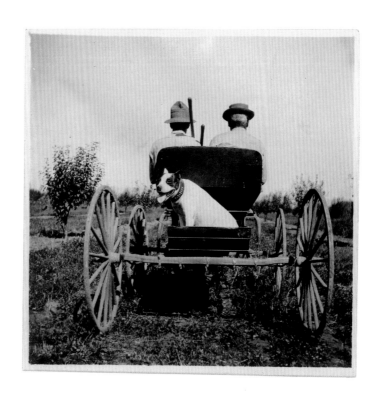

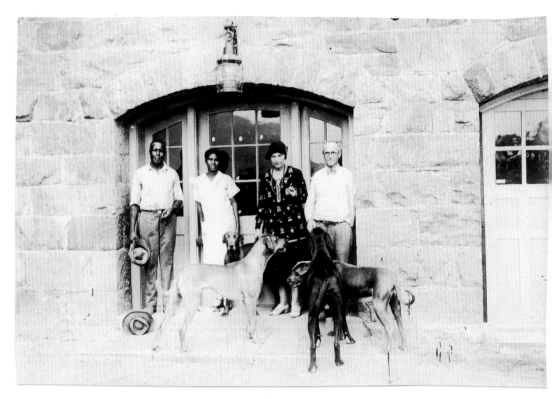

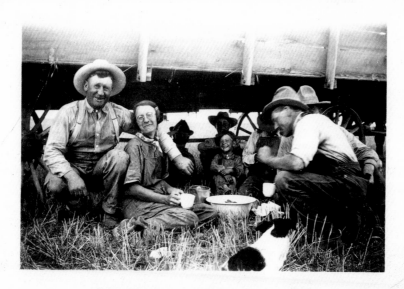

IN THE OLD DAYS

1925

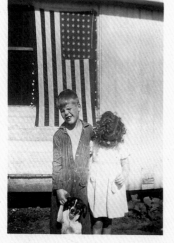

Jim Janice

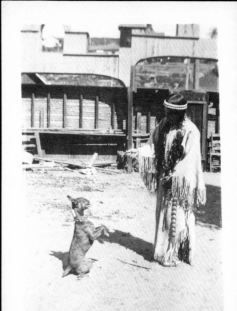

Rex

Greetings

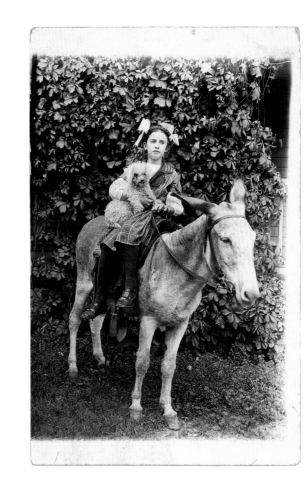
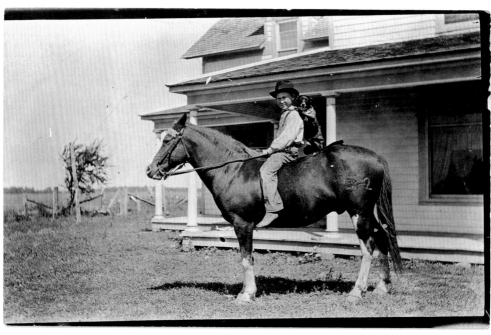

*A man, a horse and a dog never weary of each other's company.*
*— Anonymous*

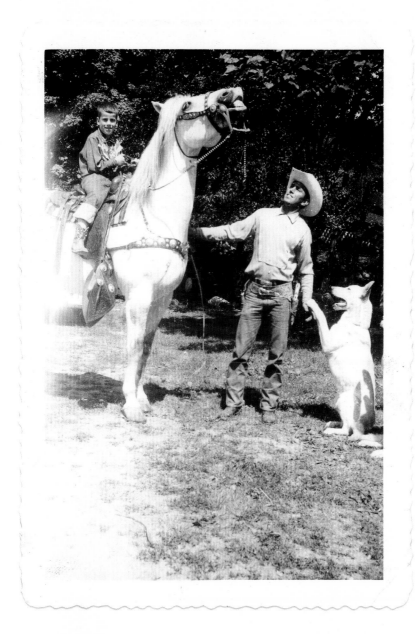

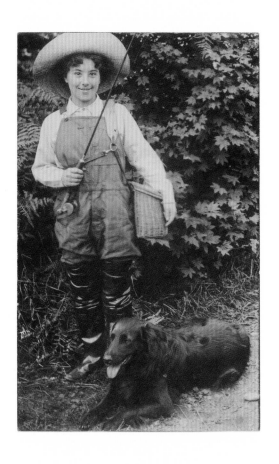

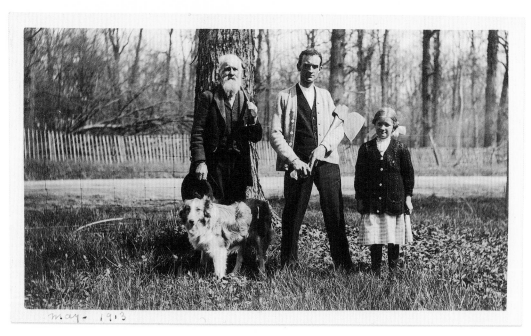

May- 1913

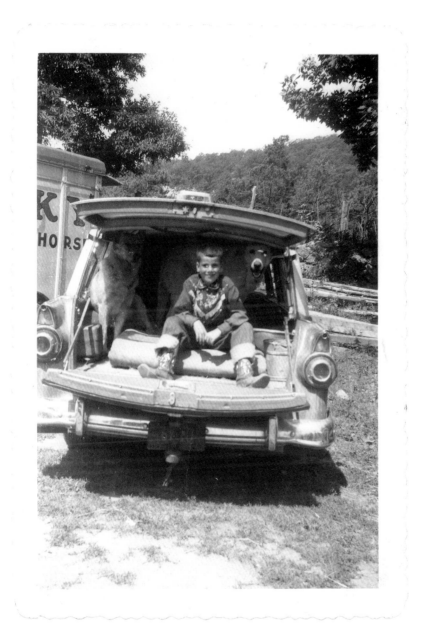

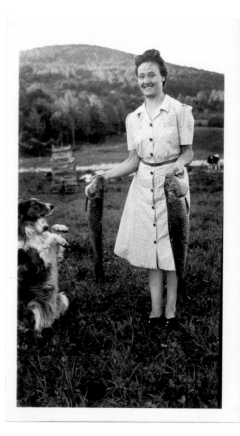

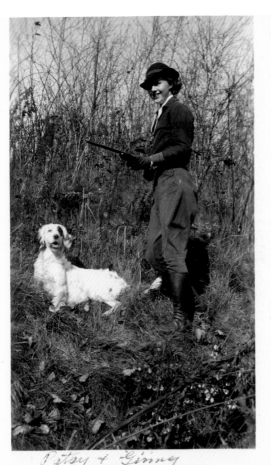

Patsey + Ginny

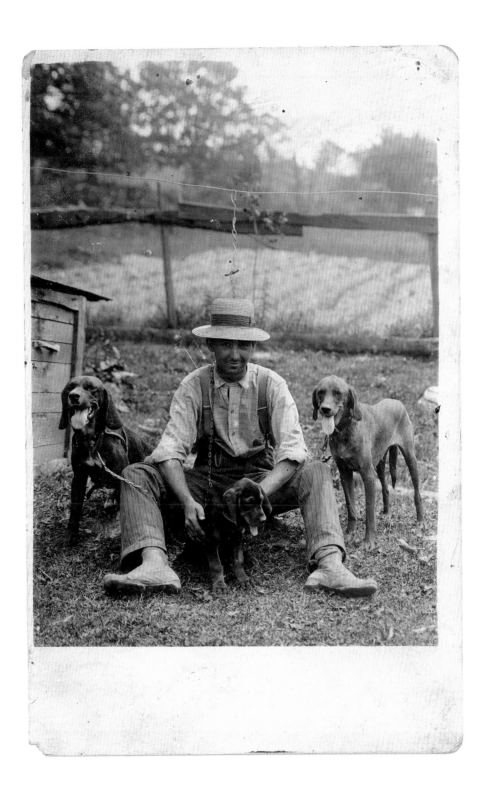

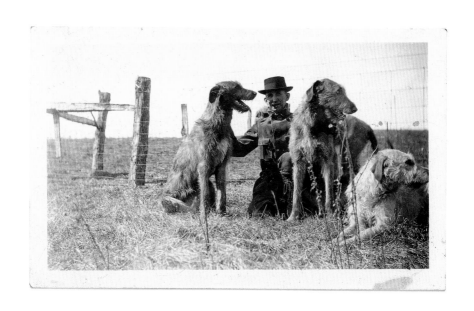

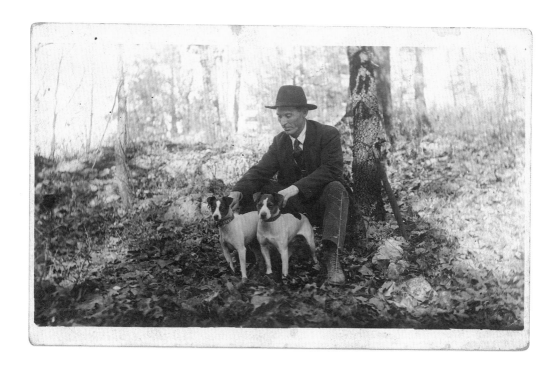

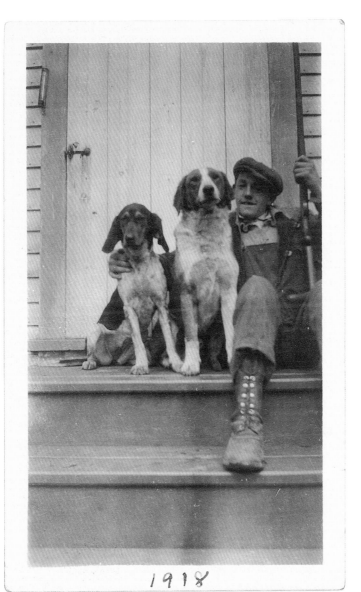

1918

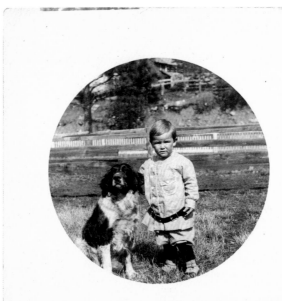

What do
you think
of my,
Boy.

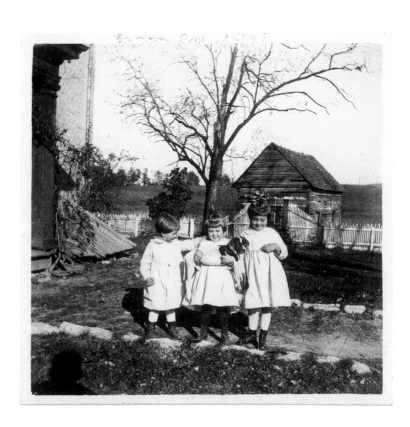

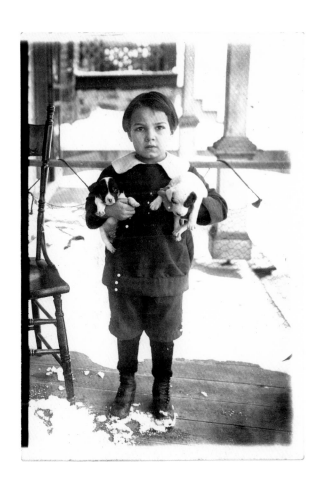
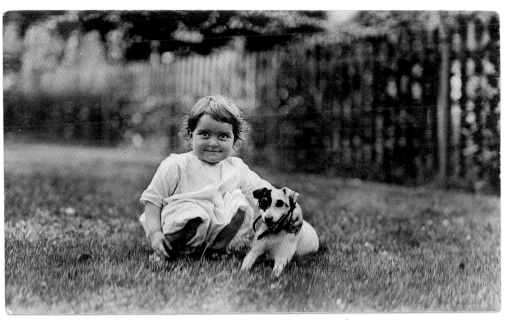

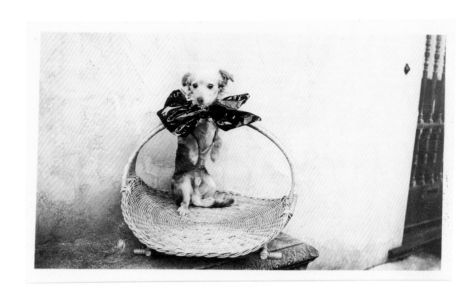

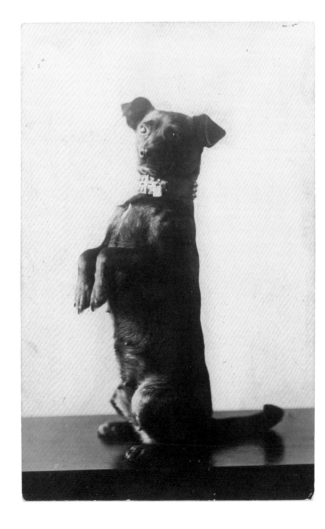

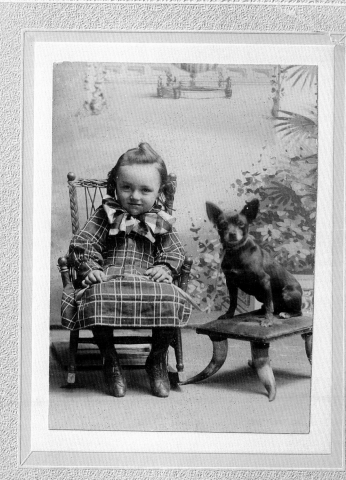

HUBBELL, - CLINTON, MO.

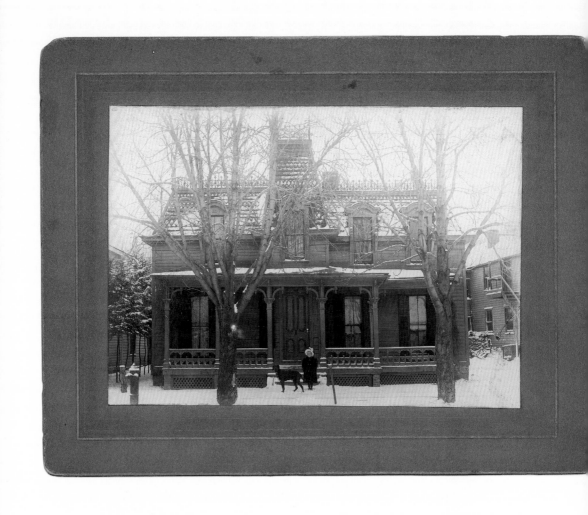

*Histories are more full of examples
of the fidelity of dogs than of friends.
— Alexander Pope*

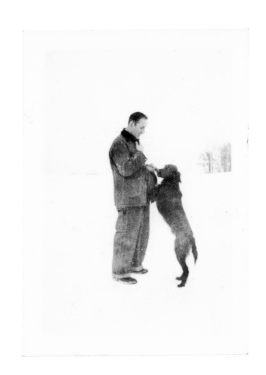

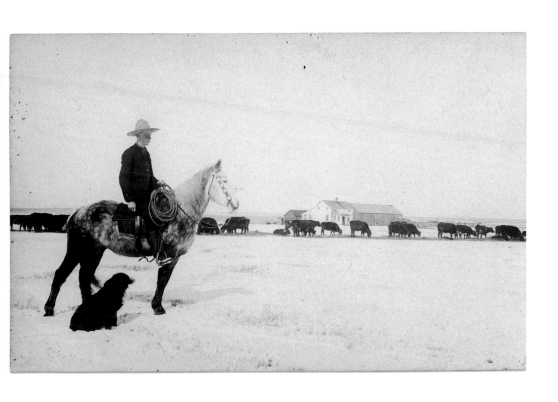

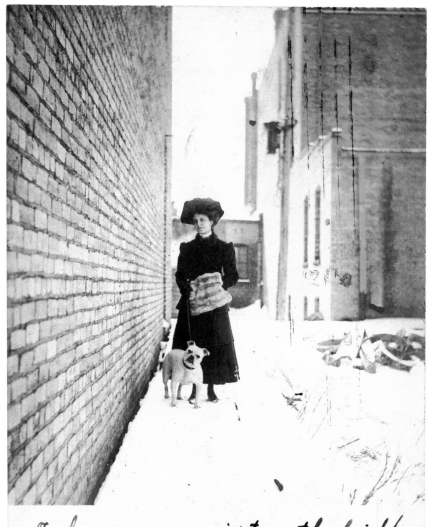

Taken on my sixteenth birthday in Fargo, N. Dakota. at
the old stage door.

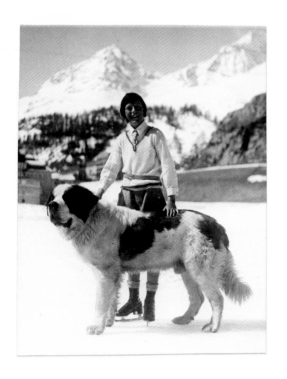

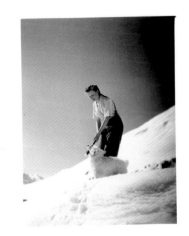

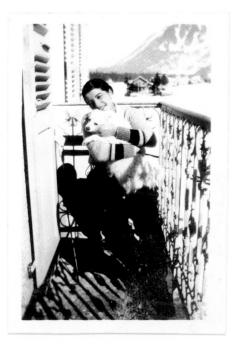

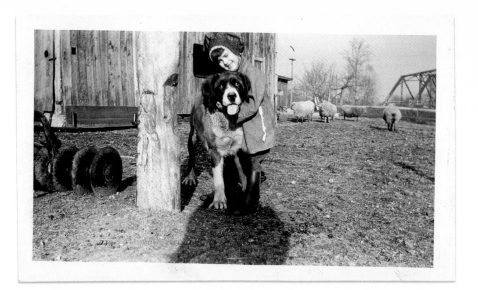

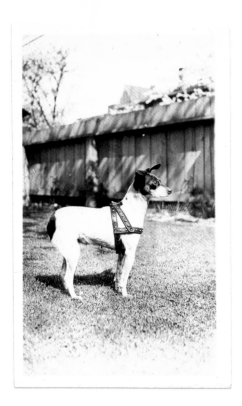

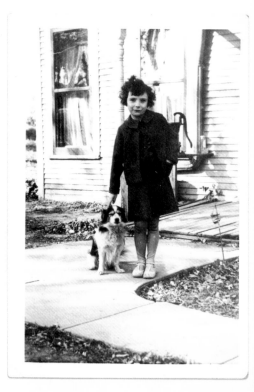

*Quite often the easiest family member to get along with is the dog.*
*— Anonymous*

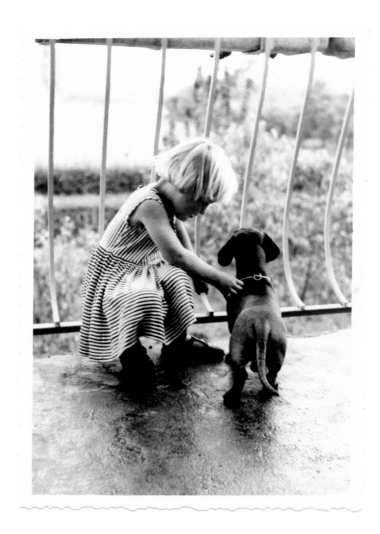

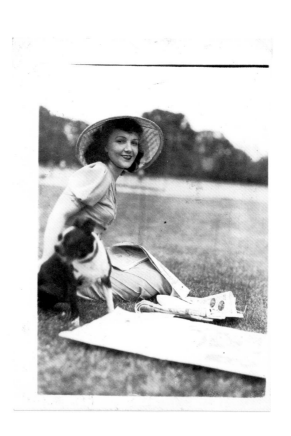

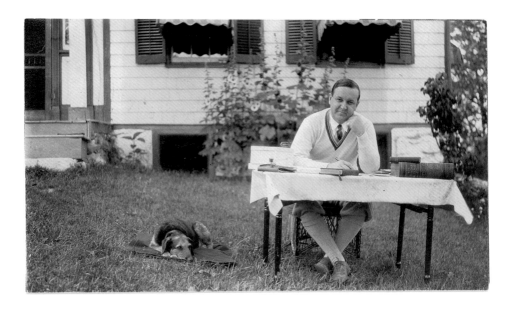

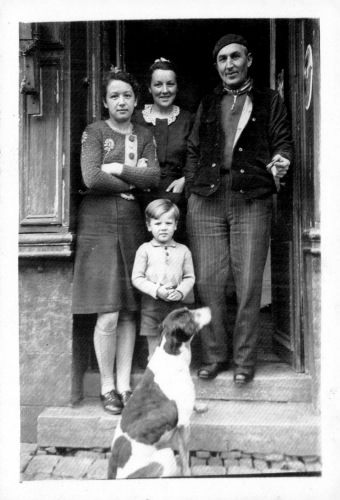

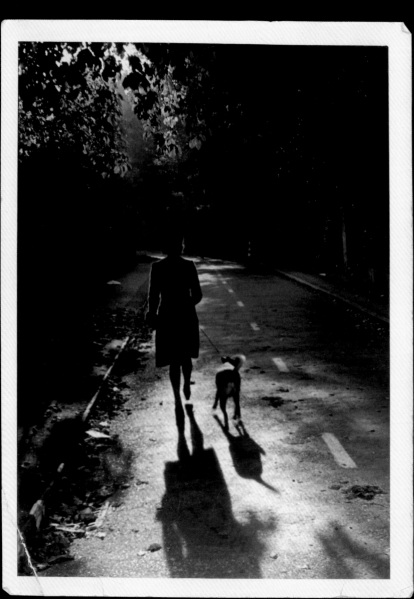

AFTERWORD

BY WILLIAM WEGMAN

What is it about dogs and the camera? I have noticed
from my own experience that there is something.

*

For amateurs and professionals alike, picture-taking
begins with a special occasion. You can see this
in Catherine Johnson's collection even as the dogs
are in the car, on top of a table, or on the front
porch with the family. They like to perform, which
may require a variety of interesting tasks
involving both photographer and subject.

*

In my own work, the idea comes first, which may require
assembling and packing of certain things of dog
interest. A favorite toy or treats perhaps. They pay
close attention. They do not want to be left behind.

*

Then there comes the search for a location. Will
this make a good background? Some exploring may be
necessary. Dogs can relate. They are hunting dogs
perhaps. What about the light? Is it too windy?
Noisy? For the effect of spontaneity, everything
needs to be just right.

Costumes may be involved and props. Something may
need to be balanced on the head: the hat that
doesn't fit (no hat fits on a dog), antlers, maybe
sunglasses. Something to smoke? How do we get that
corn cob-pipe to stay in place?

*

In those "how-to-photograph-your-dog" books they
always tell you to get low. You could do that.
Better yet find something big the dog can stand on.
Dogs want to be tall and they are often thrilled
at the challenge of balancing.

*

There may also be set construction, always
fascinating to working dogs. "Caution Men Working"
is a sign to jump in and help. The more time it
takes to take the actual picture the better.

*

Finally there are technical matters: film-loading,
light-metering, the calling out of f-stops, the
selection of lenses, tripod adjustments. All that
fiddling and muttering which subsumes the typical
shutterbug gives the dog a chance to relax (and
get their make-up on).

All dogs have their odd moments. My dog Fay needed
to be the center of attention. She didn't like to
share the stage with anyone, even houseplants.
Large metal objects didn't appeal to her much.
Her daughter Batty, on the other hand, was blasé
about it all, so relaxed on the set she looked
to be without a skeleton. Her sister Crooky was
hyper-alert. For her, photography was a state of
emergency. Now there are Bobbin, Penny and Candy.
Candy is a bit of a problem. She wants to be
included but makes a face while up there. Not that
it matters to her.

*

Dogs love everything about photography except the
photograph itself.

# ON COLLECTING

## BY CATHERINE JOHNSON

For: Glenn, Norman Parkinson,
Lula, Dixie and especially
Little Bob.

For my fifth birthday my parents
gave me an endearing and wacky
terrier I named Little Bob
(above right), a name apropos
for a diminutive dog with such a considerable
personality. Since then, I have been captivated
by the relationships between people and their dogs,
their shared bond and mutual admiration.

I've been collecting dog images since before I
could even read or write. While on our annual
family vacation in Kentucky, my mother let me
pick out a memento in a gift shop. With the small
change I had, I bought a modern 4 x 5 inch glossy
picture of a beagle. The dog was representative
of a dog that had lived in the 1800s and had been
the subject of Stephen Collins Foster's song,
*My Old Dog Tray*. Even though I was old enough

to know that photo wasn't really of Old Dog Tray,
it didn't matter. I loved that photo.

I was inspired to collect photographs of dogs
seriously many years later while working for the
legendary British photographer Norman Parkinson. He
had come back from a difficult portrait commission
of a family who neither liked to be photographed
nor liked each other. He said, "if you're shooting
a difficult family portrait, pray the family has
a dog and feature that animal front and center!"
After looking at his contact sheets, I saw he was
absolutely right: the dog infused the portrait
with energy and humour.

I began to see Parkinson's theory even in amateur
snapshots. There is something about these frozen
moments in time that make the dogs, the people and
the photographs endearing and magical. There is no
doubt that the prevalence of pet ownership today
is part of our desperate need and desire to remain
connected to the purity of the natural world.
Please adopt or donate to your local animal shelter.
They need you.

Many thanks to my friends who have encouraged me in my collecting:
Roberto Dutesco, Rebecca Johnson, Liz, Page, Ryann, and Dylan
Keating, Dr. Stanley Burns, Liz Burns, Carlos Gomez, James Crump,
Fiona Cowan, Laura Hughes, The Bibers, Anthony Petrillose, Meghan
Williams, Tara Garcia, Sarah Schulte, Kristen Roeder, Liz Tuncer,
Betsy Guerro, Andrew Cahill, Chris Chao, Christopher Sweet, David
& Sue Redding, Molly Logan, Kim Forsberg, John Szarkowski, Scott
Richards and Aldon James. Also Dr. Kuhlman and the staff at the
Gramercy Park Animal Hospital. And to my dealers and friends that
I met on eBay, Tammra Engum and Barbara Levine. And Lula, Dixie,
Ruby and Little Bob for the inspiration.

Extra thanks to my wonderful editor at Phaidon, Denise Wolff.
Thanks as well to Julia Hasting, Karen Farquhar, Samantha Woods
and Makiko Ushiba Katoh.

I would also like to thank some of the greatest photographers in
the world who have so lovingly photographed dogs and who I have
been lucky enough to meet: Bruce Weber, Elliott Erwitt and above
all William Wegman who so generously wrote a piece for this book.

Phaidon Press Limited
Regent's Wharf
All Saints Street
London N1 9PA

Phaidon Press Inc.
180 Varick Street
New York, NY 10014

www.phaidon.com

First published 2007
© 2007 Phaidon Press Limited

ISBN 978 0 7148 4803 7

A CIP catalogue record for this book is available
from the British Library.

Designed by Julia Hasting
Printed in China